NATURAL SCIENCES

CLEP* Test Study Guide

All rights reserved. This Study Guide, Book and Flashcards are protected under the US Copyright Law. No part of this book or study guide or flashcards may be reproduced, distributed or stored in a retrieval system, or transmitted in any form or by any means, electronic, mechanical, photocopying, recording, or otherwise, without the prior written permission of the publisher Breely Crush Publishing, LLC.

© 2026 Breely Crush Publishing, LLC

*CLEP is a registered trademark of the College Entrance Examination Board which does not endorse this book.

971010221143

Copyright ©2003 - 2026, Breely Crush Publishing, LLC.

All rights reserved.

This Study Guide, Book and Flashcards are protected under the US Copyright Law. No part of this publication may be reproduced, distributed or stored in a retrieval system, or transmitted in any form or by any means, electronic, mechanical, photocopying, recording, or otherwise, without the prior written permission of the publisher Breely Crush Publishing, LLC.

Published by Breely Crush Publishing, LLC
10808 River Front Parkway
South Jordan, UT 84095
www.breelycrushpublishing.com

ISBN-10: 1-61433-644-X
ISBN-13: 978-1-61433-644-0

Printed and bound in the United States of America.

*CLEP is a registered trademark of the College Entrance Examination Board which does not endorse this book.

Table of Contents

Biological Sciences *1*
   1. The Origin of Life and Evolution *1*
      The Origin of Life *1*
      Evolutions *6*
      Classifications for Organisms *7*
   2. Cell Structure and Division, Genetics and Bioenergetics and Biosynthesis *8*
      Cell Structure *8*
      Comparison of Prokaryotic and Eukaryotic Cells *12*
      Properties of Cell Membranes *12*
   3. Enzymes *14*
      Inorganic Cofactors *15*
      Roles of Coenzymes *15*
      Inhibition and Regulation *15*
   4. Energy Transformations *16*
      The Aerobic Pathway *16*
      Glycolysis and Anaerobic Pathways *17*
      Aerobic Respiration *17*
      Photosynthesis *18*
   5. Cell Division and Reproduction *18*
      Structure of Chromosomes *18*
      The Cell Cycle *19*
      Mitosis *19*
      Cytokinesis in Plants and Animals *20*
      Meiosis *20*
      Meiosis *23*
   6. Basic Gene Structure/Chemical Nature of the Gene *24*
      Watson-Crick Model of Nucleic Acids *24*
      DNA Replication *24*
      Mutations *25*
      Control of Protein Synthesis: Transcription, Translation,
         Posttranscriptional Processing *25*
      Structural and Regulatory Genes *26*
      Transformation *26*
      Viruses *26*
      Bioenergetics and Biosynthesis *28*
   7. Organism Development, Genetics, and Heredity *29*
      Organism Development *29*
      Genetics and Patterns of Heredity *29*
Animal Breeding *33*

Rh Factor 33
Albinism 33
    Population Biology: The Struggle for Existence 33
Chemical/Physical Sciences 34
  1. Atomic and Nuclear Structure 34
  2. Elements, Compounds, Reactions, and Atomic Bonds 37
  3. Thermodynamics, States of Matter, Classical Mechanics and Relativity........38
    Thermodynamics...38
    States of Matter..40
    Classical Mechanics 40
    Relativity 41
  4. Electricity and Magnetism, Light and Sound....................................42
    Electricity..42
    Magnetism 42
    Light..43
    Sound 44
  5. The Universe, Galaxies, Solar Systems, and Stars............................45
    The Universe...45
    Galaxies..45
    Solar Systems..46
    Nebular Hypothesis 46
    Stars 47
  6. The Earth..48
    Earth's Atmosphere..48
    Hydrosphere..48
    Earth's Structure..48
    Surface Features and Geological Processes 49
    Geological History of the Earth 50
    Ecosystems..51
Global Climate and the Greenhouse Effect..52
    An Introduction 52
    Our Changing Atmosphere 52
    Changing Climate..54
    Living With Uncertainty...55
    What are Greenhouse Gases?..55
    What are Emissions Inventories? 56
    What are Sinks? 56
    Pollution 56
    Environmental Risk Assessment...56
    Acid Rain 57

  How Do We Measure Acid Rain? 58
  What are Acid Rain's Effects? 59
 7. Bonus Section 59
  Photosynthesis 59
  Food Chain 59
  Prenatal Genetics Vocabulary 59
  Body Essentials 60
  Bacteria 61
  Disease 61
  Functions of the Body 62
  Temperature Regulation in Animals 63
  Endocrine System 63
  Insects 64
  Plants 64
  Flower Reproductive Parts 65
  Scientific Method 65
  Animal Breeding 65
  Rh Factor 66
  Albinism 66
  Charles Darwin 66
Physics 66
 1. The Basics of Motion 66
 2. Vectors 68
 3. The Basics of Motion 69
  Newton's Laws of Motion 69
Sample Test Questions 70
Test-Taking Strategies 116
What Your Score Means 116
Test Preparation 117
Legal Note 117
References 118

Biological Sciences

1. THE ORIGIN OF LIFE AND EVOLUTION

The origin of life on Earth has long been a hotly debated topic. Perhaps even more controversial, however, is the theory of evolution. Prior to the mid-1600s, most people believed that humans had been created by God, and that all other organisms were capable of spontaneously arising from the air, or even mud or decaying matter. During the 18th and 19th centuries, these ideas were subject to increasingly severe criticism which resulted in the foundation of the theories that still hold true to this day. In this section, we will discuss the main theories regarding the origin of life and evolution.

THE ORIGIN OF LIFE

In the mid-1800s, two important scientific advances made it increasingly more difficult for people to cling to their belief that life could spontaneously arise from next to nothing.

One of these advances was made by Louis Pasteur (1822-1895), who was known as the greatest biologist of the nineteenth century. In 1864, Pasteur discredited the idea of spontaneous generation through a simple experiment using a sterilized flask with a bent neck. In this famous experiment, Pasteur demonstrated that plain air cannot initiate the growth of microorganisms. Instead, germs must be introduced to the environment in order to grow a culture in a flask. He also demonstrated that organisms cannot come into the world without being produced by parents similar to themselves. However, by proving that organisms cannot spontaneously generate, Pasteur also raised another question: Where did the first generation of each species come from?

The second major advance, the theory of natural selection, provided a partial answer to this intriguing question. The theory of natural selection was proposed by Charles Darwin and Alfred Russel Wallace. This theory indicated that some differences between individuals in a population are inherited. When the environment changes, individuals who have the traits best suited to the change in the environment are more likely to survive and reproduce successfully while those individuals that are less suited are less likely to enjoy reproductive success. Those individuals predisposed to reproductive success will pass those positive traits on to their offspring, increasing the percentage of well-adapted individuals displaying those characteristics. If these characteristics were repeated generation after generation, natural selection would allow these well-adapted organisms to evolve into more complex organisms. So, seeing as humans are such complex organisms, Darwin and Wallace stated that we must have come from a single, simple progenitor Darwin referred to as "life's last common ancestor." This ancestor would have been the last ancestor we shared with all other forms of life on Earth.

But where did this "life's last common ancestor" come from? Well, although some of Darwin's "unofficial" correspondence indicates that he believed that the life of this single-celled organism was the result of a variety of chemical reactions, due to the religious biases of his time, when he produced his famous treatise, "On the Origin of Species" in November of 1859. Darwin indicated that the "Creator" was responsible for giving rise to the first form of life on Earth, after which evolution took over. So, his work, while revolutionary for its time, still did not fully answer how life on Earth came to be.

Since the publication of Darwin's work, various theories have been proposed on how this original single-celled organism came to be. We do know from studies of fossils that life existed on Earth 3.5 billion years ago. However, even though the fossils in question are fairly simple forms of bacteria, they were still already well-advanced, living in colonies and performing photosynthesis. So we do not know exactly how life began, but there are several ideas out there.

To understand how life began on Earth, we need to understand the environment of the Earth at the time that life arose. We can only speculate on this environment, extrapolating backward using the information recorded in the Earth's rocks and comparing that information with what we know of the formation of other planets.

It is commonly believed that the Earth was created by lots of smaller chunks and particles floating around in the interstellar cloud we refer to as the solar nebula. In fact, scientists feel that the other planets and moons in our solar system were created this way as well some 4.5 billion years ago. Because the solar nebula was so laden with hydrogen gases, scientists believe that when the Earth first formed, it also contained a lot of hydrogen and hydrogen-rich molecules such as methane, ammonia and water vapor. In fact, the environment on the Earth at that time is thought to have been very similar to today's Jupiter and Saturn.

Because the Earth had a weak gravitational field when it was first formed, most of the hydrogen molecules probably escaped during the first few hundred million years of our planet's existence. As the new Earth aged, chemical reactions would have taken place between the Earth's weak atmospheric gases and the Earth's crust, creating a milder atmosphere consisting mostly of carbon monoxide, carbon dioxide, nitrogen and water. Ultraviolet radiation from the Sun on the water molecules would have caused them to break down and release some free oxygen.

The moon affects the tides of the ocean on Earth. Each day there are two high tides and two low tides. Tides are created because the moon and the Earth are attracted to one another. Everything on Earth is able to resist this pull except water.

The tides will also change based on the position of the Sun – if the Sun and the Moon find themselves 90 degrees apart in relation to someone on Earth, then the high tides are not as high as normal. This happens because the Sun's mass uses enough gravitational force on the ocean to cancel out the Moon's pull. When this happens, the lower high tide is called a neap tide.

However, when the Sun lines up with the Moon and the Earth (Full Moon) then the Sun magnifies the tidal forces, making them even higher tides. These are called spring tides, not because they happen in spring, but because the water "springs" higher than usual.

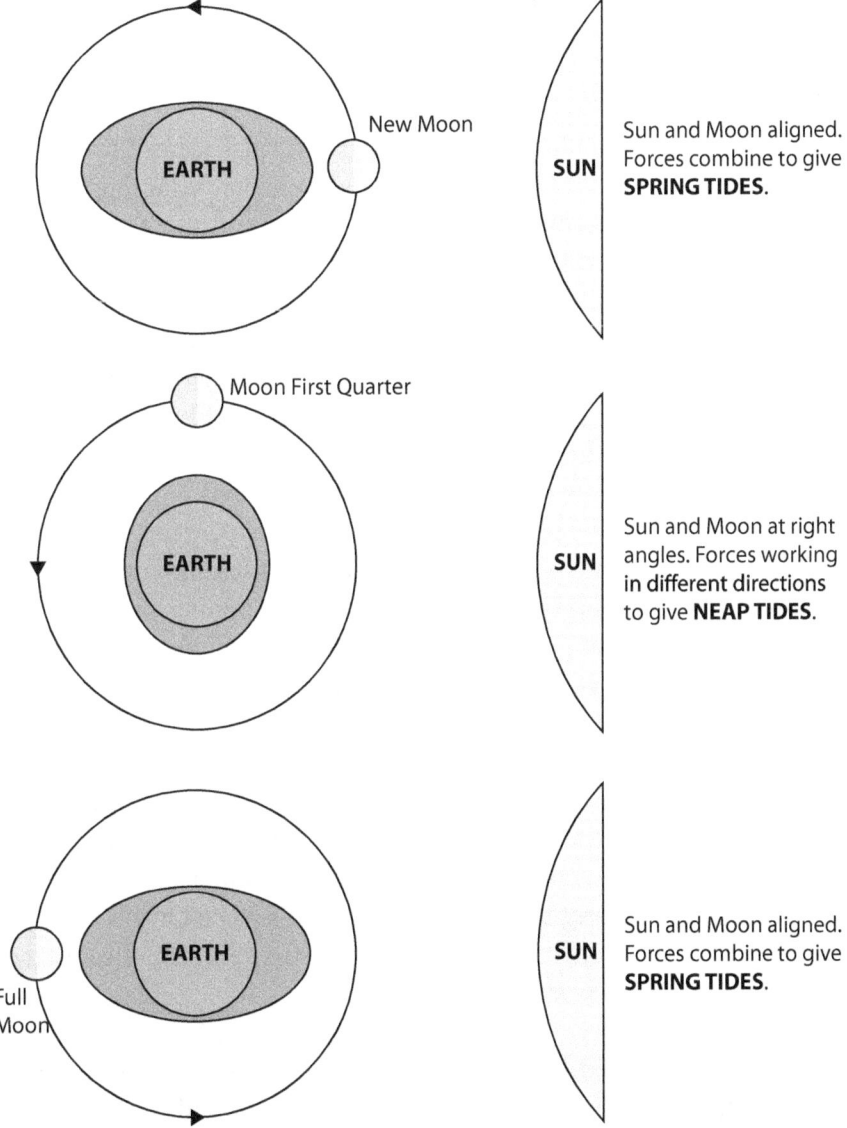

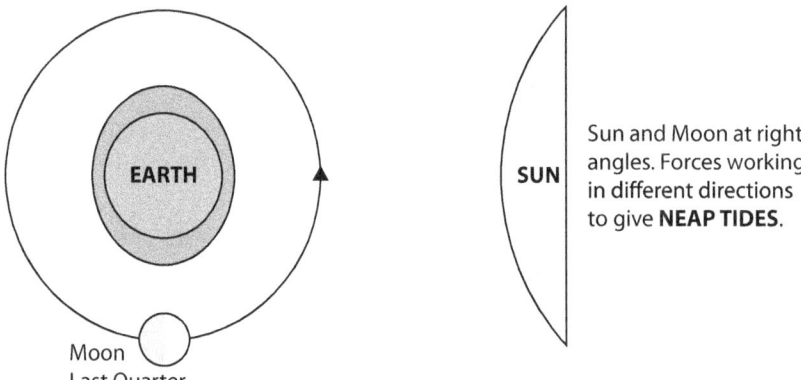

Primordial Soup Theory

The most commonly held idea for the origin of life on Earth is that the planet's early atmosphere, though extremely hostile to life today, actually facilitated the production of organic carbon-containing molecules, even as the atmosphere grew milder or was "reducing." The driving force behind the reactions creating these organic molecules would probably have been the ultraviolet radiation from the Sun, which was likely the Earth's primary energy source. However, other sources include lightning, geothermal energy such as hot springs and volcanoes, radioactivity in the Earth's crust, meteorite impact, and sub-atomic bombardment. These organic compounds would have formed in either the lower atmosphere or on the surface of the planet, then may have been washed out by rainfall into lakes, pools or ponds, all of which would have been rich in dissolved minerals from all of the chemical reactions taking place on the Earth's surface and in its new atmosphere. These areas served as protective environments and would have given the molecules the opportunity to interact at random. Some of the reactions would have produced compounds that served as guides in the formation of other molecules. The success of the formation of additional molecules would have resulted in the replication of molecules, and thus the eventual evolution of life.

This theory, dubbed the "primordial soup" theory of the origin of life, was independently developed in the 1920's by both a Scottish biologist by the name of John Haldane and a Russian biochemist named Alexander Oparin. Both Haldane and Oparin published works on the origin of life, but Haldane's "The Origin of Life," published in 1929, is the most well-known. Oparin's work was temporarily forgotten due to Russia's recovery from their civil war at the time.

Haldane's work suggested that the natural conditions on primitive Earth would facilitate the production of simple organic molecules and would lead to complexity without chemical diversity. He also indicated that these conditions, because of the many chemical reactions taking place, would facilitate the development of forms of chemical activity capable of putting life in motion and the formation of membranes around primitive cells would hold the necessary components of the cell in the proper places.

It was not until 1953 that the first part of this theory was tested. That year, an experiment performed by Stanley Miller and Harold Urey simulated the environment of a young Earth. The experiment mixed a variety of gases in a closed environment, with the gases (methane, ammonia, hydrogen and water vapor) contained in an upper chamber and water contained in a lower chamber, with the two chambers connected by a circuit of glass pipes. The whole circuit was subjected to an electrical discharge using tungsten electrodes, resulting in the formation of compounds at the bottom of the apparatus. When these compounds were analyzed, it was discovered that aldehydes, carbolic acid, and amino acids were contained within the resultant solution. The presence of these compounds, thought to be the basic chemical ingredients of life, showed that they could be formed under the simulated primitive conditions of Earth.

Other experiments similar to this one but using different chemicals have resulted in the production of amino acids. Ironically, the key behind all of these experiments seems to be the absence of oxygen, an element that is absolutely vital to our survival today.

Interstellar Theory

Other theories regarding the origin of life on Earth include theories such as that put forth by the astrophysicist Fred Hoyle, who suggested that complex organic molecules in interstellar clouds might have been responsible for the beginning of biological activity on the planet and perhaps in other areas of our galaxy as well. Hoyle feels that it is entirely possible that life developed in these interstellar clouds, and that comets may carry viruses. In fact, Hoyle feels that encounters with comets in past eras may have been responsible for plagues on Earth.

Evolution

Evolution has been a hot topic for more than three hundred years. There are two primary theories behind how humans became what they are: creationism and evolution.

Creationism

Theories of evolution and the origin of life on Earth have long been tied up with religious dogma. The traditional Judeo-Christian version of the world held that the universe and the world had been created by God, who created an infinite and continuous series of life forms, each one grading to the next from the simplest to the most complex. This theory is known as creationism.

According to the theory of creationism, man was created in his present form about 6,000 years ago, within days of the creation of all other life, and has remained largely unchanged since that time. This belief was strongly reinforced by James Ussher, a 17th century archbishop from Ireland. He was famous for having counted the generations from the Bible and adding them to modern history, allowing him to fix the date of creation at Monday, October 23, 4004 B.C. Dr. Charles Lightfoot of Cambridge University in England went one step further, proclaiming that the time of creation was at 9:00 a.m. on that date.

EVOLUTIONS

It was not until the 18th century that creationism was really questioned in great detail. Karl von Linné, better known as Carlous Linnaeus, was famed for his work in Botany. He was known for his descriptions of nature using binomial nomenclature, but until later in life, did not really question why things were the way they were, but chose to categorize them instead. However, when he was older, it bothered him that plant hybrids could be created by cross- pollination. He noted that, if all plants, like humans, had been set down perfectly by God, they should not be able to cross-pollinate or change. Despite his keen observations, though, Linnaeus stopped short of suggesting evolution, but he had paved the way for future scientists to do so.

Later in the 18th century, scientists like George Louis Leclerc, a zoologist, and Comte de Buffon, began to quietly suggest that nature is not fixed and that organisms changed through time. Buffon went a step further and suggested that this meant that the Earth must be older than simply 6,000 years, and made what was at the time an astounding hypothesis when he suggested that the Earth must be at least 75,000 years old and that humans and apes were related. Still, both Leclerc and Buffon were careful not to promote their theories in a public forum and instead publicly rejected the idea that species could evolve in order to avoid public ridicule.

Yet another late 18th century evolutionist was Erasmus Darwin, grandfather of Charles Darwin. Erasmus Darwin was another "closet-evolutionist" who believed that evolution occurred in all living things, including humans. Still, he was unsure of what caused evolution.

The first scientist to publicly state that evolution occurred was Charles Lamarck, who theorized that microscopic organisms spontaneously appear, then evolve progressively through time to produce more complex life forms until they reach perfection, which, of course, was then perceived to be humanity. Lamarck declared that this evolution was caused by the inheritance of acquired characteristics that were caused by environmental influences.

One of Lamarck's biggest opponents, George Cuvier, scoffed at the idea of inherited characteristics, but he did believe that there had been earlier life forms. In fact, he was the first scientist to document extinct species. However, Cuvier denied that evolution occurred and instead subscribed to the theory of catastrophism, stating that violent natural catastrophes resulted in various species of plants and animals being killed off. Then new forms of life moved in and took over these areas, causing the fossil record to sometimes change drastically from one time period to the next.

It took another scientist, Charles Lyell, to prove Cuvier wrong. He believed in slower, progressive changes and hypothesized that the Earth must be extremely old and had been subject to natural processes in the past that are still currently in motion and shaping the land, including erosion, earthquakes, volcanoes, and decomposition. Lyell conclusively proved that forces changing the shape of the Earth's surface must have been operating in the past much the same way as they are now, an idea referred to as uniformitarianism.

The idea of uniformitarianism was key in Darwin's understanding of biological evolution, and resulted in his theory that organisms will evolve dependent upon their surrounding environment and the organisms' natural traits, expressing traits that maximize their likelihood to live long enough to reproduce, and repressing those traits that do not. His most famous experiment involved finches from the Galápagos Islands. Darwin noted that the finches from all of the islands contained in the Galápagos Islands were not the same. Instead, many had differently shaped beaks depending upon the island that they lived on. He noted that the islands' environments were not all the same, some were very arid while others were rich and fertile. As a result, those birds on the more arid islands that had beaks more suited for eating cactus got more food, and therefore were more likely to be able to mate. Those finches ending up on one of the other, less arid islands, did not have to eat cactus and therefore did not have a beak suited to eating the plant. It appeared that nature had selected the best-adapted varieties for these birds to survive and reproduce. This process has come to be known as natural selection.

One important distinction Darwin noted is that the environment does not produce these traits within the finch population. Instead, these finches are expressing traits already existing in their genes. So, it is not the environment that causes these genes to develop; however, it is the environment that makes the expression of the genes desirable. Some of Darwin's supporters have called this process as "survival of the fittest," which is very different from Lamarck's idea of evolution, which theorized that the environment caused these traits to develop.

CLASSIFICATIONS FOR ORGANISMS

This is the scientific classification order for organisms:
1. Kingdom
2. Phylum (animals) or Division (plants)
3. Class
4. Order
5. Family
6. Genus
7. Species

For Humans, the complete classification is as follows in bold:

1. Kingdom **Animalia**
2. Phylum (animals) or Division (plants) **Chordata**
3. Class **Mammalia**
4. Order **Primates**
5. Family **Hominidae**
6. Genus **Homo**
7. Species **Sapiens**

For dogs, the complete classification is as follows in bold:
1. Kingdom **Animalia**
2. Phylum (animals) or Division (plants) **Chordata**
3. Class **Mammalia**
4. Order **Carnivora**
5. Family **Canidae**
6. Genus **Canis**
7. Species **C. lupus**

Animals with a spinal cord are called cordata. A phylogenic tree is something that predicts probable evolution.

Homologous structures: similar bone structures. A human arm is similar to other mammals' arms, like a monkey's.

2. CELL STRUCTURE AND DIVISION, GENETICS AND BIOENERGETICS AND BIOSYNTHESIS

CELL STRUCTURE

All living organisms are made up of a conglomeration of cells. The first cells on Earth were likely prokaryotes, or cells with no nucleus or center. It is thought that eukaryotes, cells with a nucleus, did not develop until nearly 2.5 billion years ago with the transition of the Earth from a sparsely oxygenated environment to an oxygen-rich environment. This section is an overview of cell structure and basic bioenergetics and biosynthesis. Here we will discuss the overall structure of cells, moving from the general to the specific.

As we all know, all plants and animals are made up of a conglomeration of different types of cells. The structure of a cell will vary depending upon its function; however, all cells contain the following components.

Cell membrane. All cells have a cell membrane. Simply put, the membrane holds all the stuff that is supposed to be in the cell inside the cell. However, cell membranes are permeable in that they allow small particles, such as proteins, water, and waste, to move in and out of the cell.

Cytoplasm. This salty, jelly-like goo is found within the cell membrane and holds the nucleus in eukaryotes, plus all other cellular components within the cell membrane. The function of the cytoplasm is to protect and support the components within.

Ribosomes. These are free-floating in prokaryotes, and attached to the endoplasmic reticulum (also referred to as the E.R., this organelle is a tiny network of tubes or membranes used to transfer materials throughout the cell) in eukaryotes. Their function is to produce protein.

Mitochondrion. Mitochondria are tiny bean-shaped cellular components responsible for breaking down sugars entering the cell into energy. Within these small structures are yet more membranes, known as cristae. We will discuss mitochondria in even more detail later when we discuss bioenergetics.

Now that you have an idea of what all cells have in common, let's discuss the cell differences. Cells are broken down into two basic types: eukaryotes and prokaryotes. Eukaryotes are found in humans and other multi-cellular organisms such as other animals, plants, algae and protozoa. Prokaryotes are found in bacteria and cyanophytes (photosynthetic bacteria).

There are several differences between the two types. Most significantly, prokaryotes, or bacteria, have no membrane containing the nucleus of the cell. Instead, their genetic materials, composed of a circular DNA, are contained in the cytoplasm rather than in a nucleus. A typical prokaryotic structure includes appendages, or attachments to the cell surface, in the form of flagella and pili (the flagella propel the prokaryotic cell; the pili mediate the transfer of DNA between cells); a cell envelope comprised of a capsule, cell wall and plasma membrane (all of which work together to hold the cell together); and an area filled with cytoplasm containing the cell genome (DNA) and ribosomes, plus a variety of inclusions. These inclusions can be anything from additional nutrients kept in reserve or materials that make the prokaryotic cell unique from other prokaryotic cells.

Prokaryotes are far more prevalent than eukaryotes, as they are extremely adaptable. Because of its adaptability, bacteria is found in many forms in virtually any environment.

Eukaryotes are far more complex than prokaryotes. The name eukaryote means "true nut" in Greek. This definition refers to the nucleus of eukaryotic cells. Another differentiating feature of eukaryotic cells is that eukaryotes have a cytoskeleton. This cytoskeleton is actually a network of protein filaments, primarily actin and tubulin, which are anchored to the cell membrane and crisscross the cell's periphery. The cytoskeleton provides the cell its shape, stabilizing its membrane systems and permitting the cell to exert tension on the membrane, allowing it to move. Because these cells can contract, they are responsible for muscle function and the operation of the apparatus separation cells during mitosis.

Another thing eukaryotes have that prokaryotes do not is the endoplasmic reticulum or E.R. The base structure of this organelle is similar to the cell's plasma membrane; however, it is an extension of the nuclear membrane, or the sac that contains all the information held in the nucleus. The E.R. transports proteins that are to become part of the cell membrane, as well as proteins that are to be excreted from the cell in the form of waste. There are two different types of E.R.: rough and smooth. The smooth E.R. is where lipids, or fats and oils, form. It is also the site where cells excrete toxins. Rough E.R. is where proteins are transported and formed. This type of E.R. is studded with ribosomes, which synthesize energy.

Eukaryotes also have flagella, appendages used to propel the organism through liquid; however, the eukaryote's flagellum is entirely different from that of a prokaryote. Many scientists describe these flagellum as "undulipodium" in order to emphasize their completely different structure. These flagellum or undulipodium are actually composed of a bundle of nine pairs of microtubules surrounding a central pair. The base of the eukaryotic flagella holds a "microtubule organizing center," or MTOC. In animals MTOCs also serve to pull the cell's chromosomes apart during cell division, or mitosis.

Eukaryotes are further broken down to two types: plant cells and animal cells. Plant cells contain a nucleolus in the nucleus that manufactures ribosomes, which later move out of the nucleus to attach themselves to plant cells' rough E.R. They also contain a centrosome within the nucleus, which divides to produce two centrosomes at opposite ends of the nucleus during cell reproduction. The Golgi apparatus is located within the cell membrane outside of the nucleus in the cytoplasm and assists in the transport of macromolecules throughout the cell. Also within the Golgi apparatus are the enzymatic or hormonal contents of lysosomes (which are somewhat rare in plants, but assist in intercellular digestion), peroxisomes (which protect the cells from their own production of hydrogen peroxide) and secretory vesicles (which release hormones and neurotransmitters). Also contained within the plant cell are vacuoles that mediate what is called turgor pressure in the cell. For example, if a plant is well watered, the cells become rigid, causing the plant to become rigid. Without sufficient water, though, the pressure within the cells is reduced and the plant droops.

The most unique thing about plant cells is that they can manufacture their own food through photosynthesis. Most plants contain chlorophyll (which makes them appear green), which permits them to use sunlight to convert water and carbon dioxide into sugars and carbohydrates. They also contain chloroplasts, or small organelles that work with chlorophyll to change light to energy. Plant cells are also unique from animal cells in that they do not use centrioles or organelles for locomotion (i.e., flagella). Also, plant cells have a single large vacuole, which acts as a water reservoir and a plasmodesmata which allows cytoplasmic substances to pass directly from cell to cell.

Animal cells are somewhat different from plant cells in that they have no cell wall, which allows animal cells to diversify even more into different tissue cells, such as muscle, bone, nerves and other cells. Additionally, animal tissues are bound to each other by a triple helix of proteins that form collagen, unlike plant and fungus cells, which are bound together by pectin. No other organisms except animals use collagen in this manner.

Prokaryotic Cell

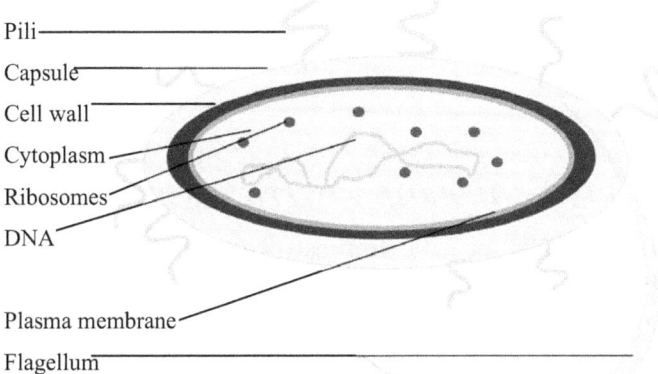

Generalized Eurkaryotic (Animal) Cell

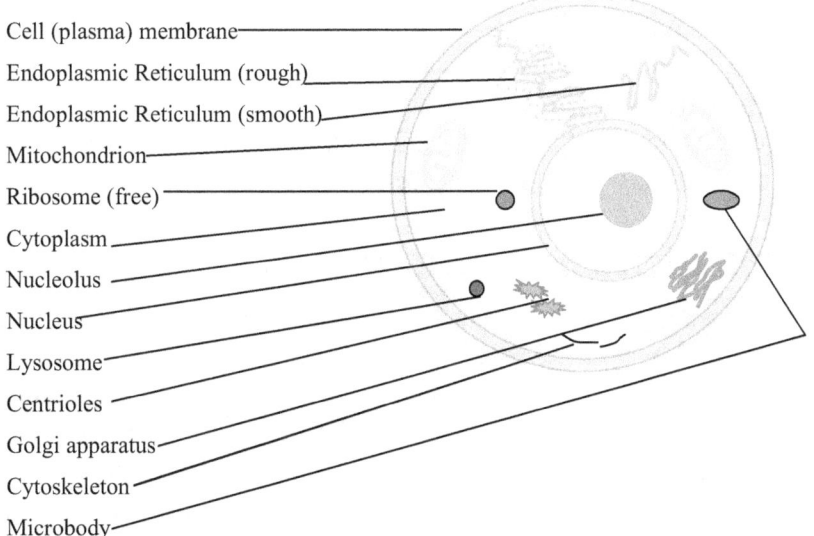

Generalized Eukaryotic (Plant) Cell

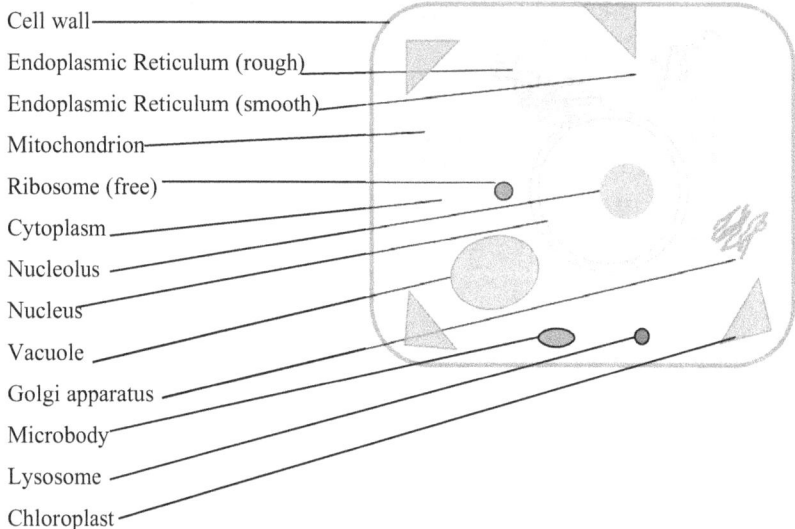

- Cell wall
- Endoplasmic Reticulum (rough)
- Endoplasmic Reticulum (smooth)
- Mitochondrion
- Ribosome (free)
- Cytoplasm
- Nucleolus
- Nucleus
- Vacuole
- Golgi apparatus
- Microbody
- Lysosome
- Chloroplast

COMPARISON OF PROKARYOTIC AND EUKARYOTIC CELLS

Prokaryotic cells are the simplest organisms. They are small and encased by a cell membrane and a rigid cell wall. Since they lack membrane-bounded organelles, all cytoplasmic constituents have access to all areas of the cell. There is usually no true nucleus. The plasma membrane carries out some of the functions organelles perform in eukaryotic cells. Some prokaryotes are propelled by a rotating flagellum. Prokaryotes cause disease, and are involved in many industrial processes. There are two main groups of prokaryotes: archaebacteria and bacteria.

Eukaryotic cells have no cell wall; however, they have an extensive endomembrane system that creates a highly compartmentalized cell with numerous membrane-bounded organelles that carry out specialized functions. Plant cells normally contain a large central vacuole (for storage) and thick cell walls. Animal cells often secrete an extracellular matrix of glycoproteins to help coordinate the behavior of all the cells in a tissue.

PROPERTIES OF CELL MEMBRANES

Basically all cells have a cell membrane. The plasma membrane, composed of a phospholipid bilayer, encloses a cell and separates its contents from its surroundings. The phospholipid bilayer impedes the passage of any water-soluble substances through it since the nonpolar tails are oriented away from water and the polar heads are oriented toward the water causing hydrogen bonding to hold the membrane together. Transport proteins in the plasma membrane help molecules and ions move into and out of the cell. The cell membrane also contains receptor proteins which induce changes in the cell when the cell comes in contact with specific molecules and markers that identify the cell. Passive transport across membranes moves down the concentration gradient. Passive transport processes include diffusion to move oxygen into cells, facilitated diffusion to move glucose into cells, and osmosis of water into cells placed in a hypotonic solution. Bulk transport utilizes endocytosis and exocytosis. Active transport, the movement of a solute across the membrane against the concentration gradient, requires the use of highly selective protein carriers and the expenditure of ATP for energy.

Structure and function of cell organelles in cells and whether they are found in Prokaryotic (Pro), or Eurkaryotic [Animal (An), and Plant (Plt)] cells

Structure	Function	Pro	An	Plt
Cell wall	Protection; support	Yes	No	Yes
Cytoskeleton	Structural support; cell movement		yes	
Flagella (cilia)	Motility or moving fluids over surfaces	Maybe	Maybe	Mostly absent
Plasma Membrane	Regulates what passes into and out of cell; cell to cell recognition	Yes	Yes	Yes
Endoplasmic Reticulum (ER)	Forms compartments and vesicles; participates in protein and lipid synthesis	No	Yes	Yes
Centrioles	Help assemble microtubules	No	Yes	No
Nucleus	Control center of cell; directs protein synthesis and cell reproduction	No	Yes	Yes
Golgi Apparatus	Packages proteins for export from cell; forms secretory vesicles	No	Yes	Yes
Lysosomes	Digest worn-out organelles and cell debris; play role in cell death	No	Yes	Yes
Microbodies	Isolate particular chemical activities from rest of cell	No	Yes	Yes
Mitochondria	Site of oxidative metabolism	No	Yes	Yes
Chloroplasts	Site of photosynthesis	No	No	Yes
Chromosomes	Contain hereditary information	Single circle	Many	Many
Nucleolus	Assemble ribosomes	No	Yes	Maybe
Ribosomes	Site of protein synthesis	Yes	Yes	Yes
Vacuoles	Storage compartment for water, sugars, ions, pigments	No	No	Yes

3. ENZYMES

Enzyme-Substrate Complex

Enzymes act as catalysts in biological processes. Most enzymes are globular proteins with one or more three-dimensional active sites where a specific substrate can bind, forming an enzyme-substrate complex. The 3D shape of the enzyme enables it to stabilize a temporary association between substrates. Either by bringing two substrates together in a correct orientation or by stressing particular chemical bonds of a substrate, the enzyme lowers the activation energy needed for the new bonds to form. Once the bonds of the substrates are broken, or new bonds are formed, the substrates convert to products. These products then dissociate from the enzyme. The reaction can then proceed much more quickly and with much less energy than would have been needed without the enzyme.

Example:

Step 1: The substrate, sucrose, consists of glucose and fructose bonded together and the enzyme has a very specifically-shaped active site.

Step 2: The substrate binds to the enzyme to form an enzyme-substrate complex.

Step 3: Stress is placed on the glucose-fructose bond in sucrose; the bond breaks and the products, glucose and fructose, are released; the enzyme is unaffected and becomes free to bind to another sucrose.

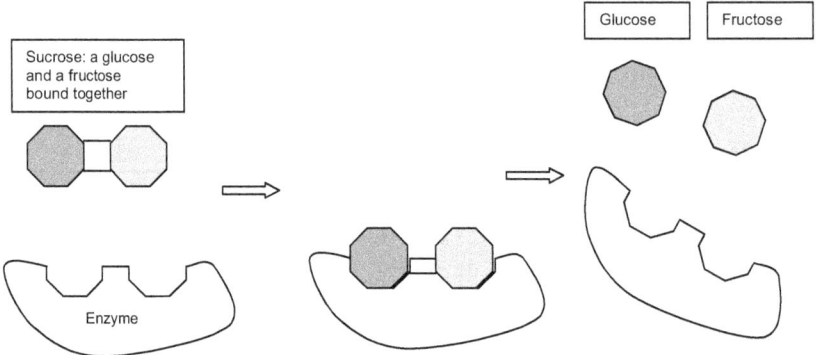

Factors affecting enzyme activity are concentration of the enzyme, concentration of the substrate, temperature, pH, salt concentration, and the binding of specific regulatory molecules. Many reactions are multi-step so are better facilitated using multi-enzyme complexes that are non-covalently bonded assemblies of enzymes that catalyze different steps of the sequence. Not all biological catalysts are proteins; RNA itself can act as a catalyst in certain types of reactions.

INORGANIC COFACTORS

The activity of enzymes is often facilitated by cofactors which can be metal ions or other substances. The active sites of many enzymes contain metal ions such as zinc, molybdenum, and manganese to help draw electrons away from substrate molecules. This makes the bonds less stable and easier to break. These metals and many vitamins are required in the diet so that they are present to play their roles.

ROLES OF COENZYMES

Cofactors that are nonprotein organic molecules are called coenzymes. Coenzymes often shuttle hydrogen ions (H+) from one enzyme to another in a cell. In oxidation reduction reactions catalyzed by enzymes, a pair of electrons passes from the enzyme to the coenzyme that becomes the electron acceptor. The coenzyme passes the electrons to a different enzyme which releases them (plus energy) to a substrate in another reaction.

A good example of this is the coenzyme nicotinamide adenine dinucleotide (NAD+). The NAD+ is composed of NMP (nicotinamide monophosphate) and AMP (adenine monophosphate) joined phosphate-to-phosphate. AMP acts as the core and provides a shape recognized by many enzymes. NMP contributes a site that accepts electrons (is reduced). NAD+ + 2 electrons + 1 proton à NADH. The energy of NADH is transferred to other molecules when the C-H bonds are broken.

INHIBITION AND REGULATION

A substance that binds to an enzyme and decreases its activity is called an inhibitor. If the end product of a biochemical pathway acts as an inhibitor of an earlier reaction in the pathway, that product is a feedback inhibitor. Competitive inhibitors compete with the substrate for the same active site; noncompetitive inhibitors bind to the enzyme in a location other than the active site. Competitive inhibitors displace substrate molecules from the enzyme by already being bound to the active site while noncompetitive inhibitors cause the enzyme to change shape which changes the shape of the active site. Many noncompetitive inhibitors bind to the enzyme location called an allosteric site which serves as a chemical active/inactive switch. Allosteric inhibitors bind to an allosteric site and reduce the enzyme activity while activators bind to an allosteric site and increase the enzyme activity.

Biochemical pathways are a series of steps which are coordinated and regulated by a cell. The product of one step becomes the substrate for the next step. If an excess of one of the products is made, it may bind to an allosteric site on an enzyme that catalyzes an earlier reaction to slow (or stop) the reaction, causing feedback inhibition.

$$E_1\ E_2\ E_3\ E_4\ E_5$$
$$A \rightarrow B \rightarrow C \rightarrow D \rightarrow E \rightarrow P$$

4. ENERGY TRANSFORMATIONS

THE AEROBIC PATHWAY

In aerobic (with oxygen) respiration, the cell gains energy from glucose molecules in a sequence of four stages: glycolysis, pyruvate oxidation, the Krebs cycle, and the electron transport chain. Oxygen is the final electron acceptor.

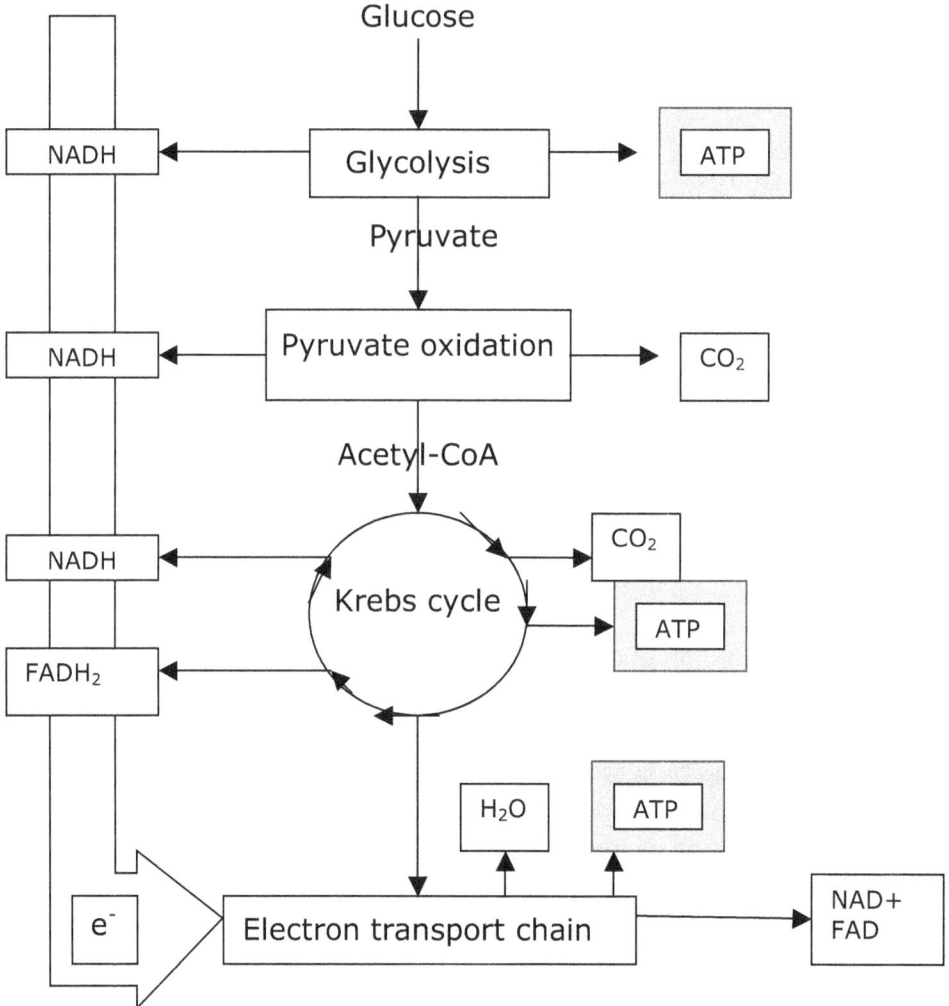

Aerobic prokaryotes and the mitochondria of eukaryotes produce the vast majority of their ATP energy by aerobic respiration in which a proton gradient formed from electrons harvested from organic molecules are donated to oxygen.

GLYCOLYSIS AND ANAEROBIC PATHWAYS

Stage one of aerobic respiration and the only stage of anaerobic respiration is glycolysis, a 10-reaction biochemical pathway. It uses substrate-level phosphorylation in the cytoplasm of the cell. In the process two ATP's are used up, but four ATP's are produced for each glucose molecule that is catabolized. Thus, the net oxidation (catabolism) of glucose is represented as:

$$C_6H_{12}O_6 + 6\ O_2 \rightarrow 2\ \text{pyruvate molecules} + 6\ H_2O + 2\ \text{ATP (energy)}$$

In the absence of oxygen, anaerobic respiration continues into lactic acid or ethanol fermentation. Examples of ethanol fermentation are yeast bread, beer, and wine. Lactic acid fermentation takes place in muscles and contributes to muscle fatigue when the resulting lactate cannot be removed fast enough by the blood.

AEROBIC RESPIRATION

Aerobic respiration involves pyruvate oxidation (stage two), the Krebs cycle (stage three), and the electron transport chain (stage four). Pyruvate, the end product of glycolysis, passes through the outer mitochondrial membrane where CO2 is split off of the pyruvate to make an acetyl group and Vitamin C is turned into Coenzyme-A. The acetyl group and Coenzyme-A combine to form acetyl-CoA, releasing NADH and a proton (H+).

$$\text{Pyruvate} + NAD^+ + CoA \rightarrow \text{acetyl-CoA} + NADH + H^+ + CO_2$$

One molecule of NAD^+ is reduced to NADH to carry electrons to be used to make ATP.

Acetyl-CoA feeds into a multi-step-reaction cycle in the Krebs cycle (citric acid cycle) where two more ATPs are extracted by phosphorylation and a large number of electrons are removed by reduction of NAD^+ to NADH.

$$\text{Acetyl-CoA} + \text{oxaloacetate} + FAD + ADP + 3\ NAD^+ \rightarrow$$
$$2\ CO_2 + 3\ NADH2^+ + ATP + FADH2$$

Remember that each glucose yields two pyruvates, thus two Acetyl-CoA molecules, so the resultant energy per glucose molecule at the end of the Krebs cycle is 6 $NADH2^+$ (12 electrons), 2 FADH2, and 2 ATP.

In the electron transport chain, $NADH2^+$ starts a chain of electron transfers that end up producing ATPs. A series of steps in the inner membrane of the mitochondria release energy to make O2 and to pump protons across the membrane. The resulting proton gradient is used by ATP synthase and ADP to produce ATP. The end result of aerobic respiration is 36 ATPs, 34 more than glycolysis alone (anaerobic respiration).

$$C_6H_{12}O_6 + 6\ O_2 \rightarrow 2\ CO_2 + 6\ H_2O + 36\ ATP\ (energy)$$

The relative levels of ADP and ATP regulate the catabolism of glucose at a key reaction of glycolysis and a key reaction of the Krebs cycle using feedback inhibition.

PHOTOSYNTHESIS

There are two phases of photosynthesis. One is the light phase which uses the chlorophyll in the chloroplast of a plant cell. The chloroplast gives plants their green color. Cells containing chlorophyll use photosynthesis to make food out of nonliving materials which serves as the support for all animal life. The light phase changes sunlight energy into chemical energy in the form of ATP and NADPH which are used to split water in hydrogen and oxygen. The oxygen is set free and becomes the oxygen all animals need to breathe. The hydrogen is retained and used in the dark phase to combine with carbon dioxide in a process known as carbon fixation to form a simple sugar like glucose. By products include starch, plant oils, and proteins. The summary equation for photosynthesis is:

$$6\ CO_2 + 6\ H_2O + light + chlorophyll \rightarrow C_6H_{12}O_6\ (glucose) + O_2$$

Anaerobic photosynthesis evolved in the absence of oxygen. Instead of reshuffling chemical bonds (in glycolysis) some organisms use light to pump protons out of their cells and use the resulting proton gradient to power the production of ATP through chemiosmosis. These organisms use H S present in the oceans as a source of hydrogen atoms. (see anaerobic respiration)

5. CELL DIVISION AND REPRODUCTION

STRUCTURE OF CHROMOSOMES

The nucleus contains various bodies called chromosomes. They may be threadlike, rod like, or have a number of other shapes. They contain chromatin, a complex of 40% DNA and 60% protein, which contains the determiners of heredity (genes). A gene is a small mass of nucleoprotein. A human has 46 chromosomes, while chimpanzees have 48. Goldfish have 94 chromosomes. This shows that chromosomes are not linked to intelligence. The particular array of all of the chromosomes an individual possesses is called its karyotype. By definition, the number of chromosomes in a species is the number of one complete set of chromosomes, the haploid (n) number. The normal number of chromosomes in a cell of a given species is the diploid (2n) number. An animal usually receives one paternal and one maternal chromosome.

THE CELL CYCLE

The cell cycle consists of five phases: G, the primary growth phase; S, the replication phase; G, the second growth phase; mitosis (comprised of prophase, metaphase, anaphase, and telophase); and cytokinesis. Interphase is the time between cell divisions. It includes the G phase which occurs after cell division and before DNA replication and occupies more than half the cell cycle. The S phase, also part of interphase, is when the cell's DNA is copied. And the G2 phase, the third part of interphase, occurs after the DNA is synthesized and before cell division. At any given time, the majority of cells in an animal's body are in the G phase which is a resting state.

MITOSIS

Mitosis is the division of the nucleus during the four phase cell division to form two identical daughter cells. When accompanied by cytokinesis, the two identical daughter cells are fully formed. The four phases of mitosis are prophase, metaphase, anaphase, and telophase.

At the start of prophase, there is a shortening and tight coiling of the DNA into rod-shaped chromosomes. The two copies of each chromosome (called chromatids) stay connected to each other by the centromere. The nucleus and nucleolus membranes break down and disappear. Centrosomes (two pairs of dark spots) appear next to the disappearing nucleus. In animal cells, each centrosome contains a pair of small cylindrical bodies called centrioles (not found in plant cells). As centrosomes separate and move toward opposite poles of cell, spindle fibers made of microtubules radiate from the centrosomes (now called mitotic spindle) in preparation for mitosis. Kinetochore fibers are attached to a disk-shaped protein called a kinetochore that is found in the centromere region of each chromosome and extend from the kinetochore of each chromatid to one of the centrosomes. Polar fibers extend across the dividing cell from centrosome to centrosome.

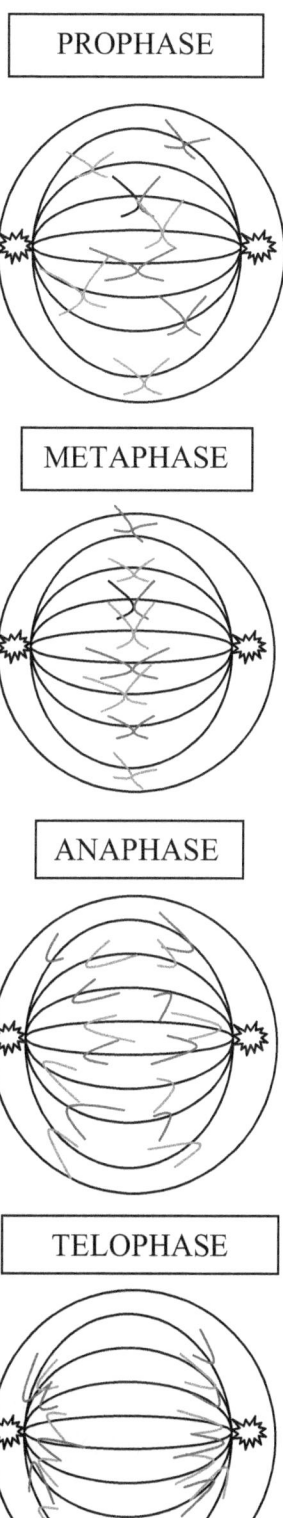

During metaphase the chromosomes are easier to identify; karyotypes are typically made from photomicrographs of chromosomes in metaphase. Kinetochore fibers move the chromosomes to the center of the dividing cell and hold them in place there along a perceived metaphase plate at the equator of the cell.

The anaphase stage is the shortest, but most beautiful. It starts when all the chromosomes di- vide simultaneously. Then the two chromatids of each chromosome separate at the centromere and slowly move, centromere first, toward the opposite poles where their kinetochores are attached. Two forms of movement take place simultaneously, each driven by microtubules: the poles move apart and the centromeres move toward the poles as the microtubules that connect them shorten. The microtubules are progressively disassembled, pulling the chromatids even closer to the poles of the cell. When the sister chromatids separate in anaphase, the essential element of mitosis – accurate partitioning of the replicated genome – is complete.

In telophase, after the chromosomes reach opposite ends of the cell, the spindle fibers disassemble. The microtubules break down to be re-used to construct the cytoskeletons of the daughter cells. A nuclear envelope forms around each set of chromosomes and the chromosomes begin to uncoil to permit gene expression. An early group of genes to be expressed is the rRNA, prompting the nucleolus to reappear. Mitosis is complete at the end of telophase.

CYTOKINESIS IN PLANTS AND ANIMALS

The cytoplasm of the cell divides in a process called cytokinesis. While mitosis was in progress the cytoplasmic organelles were re-aligned to give at least one to each daughter cell. In animal cells, cytokinesis begins with the microfilaments pinching the cell membrane inward midway between the dividing cell's two poles (cleavage furrow). In plant cells, the vesicles formed by the Golgi apparatus fuse at the midline of the dividing cell, forming a membrane-bound cell wall called the cell plate.

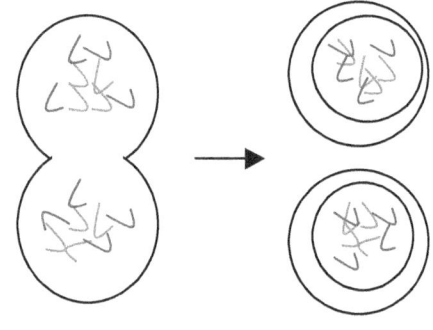

The two offspring cells are approximately same size. Each receives an identical copy of the original cell's chromosomes and approximately half of the original cell's cytoplasm and organelles.

MEIOSIS

Meiosis is the process of nuclear division that reduces the number of chromosomes in new cells to half the number in the original cell. In humans, meiosis produces haploid reproductive cells called gametes. Cells undergo the G, S and G phases of interphase so that the cell grows to a mature size and copies its DNA. Cells undergoing meiosis divide twice so one diploid cell (2n) becomes 4 haploid cells (1n). Meiosis in diploid organisms has Meiosis I and Meiosis II, each with prophase, metaphase, anaphase, telophase and cytokinesis. The purpose of Meiosis I is to produce two cells, each of which has half the number of chromosomes (but each chromosome has two chromatids). Meiosis II has no copying of the DNA. The purpose of Meiosis II is to create a total of four cells, each with a single chromatid of each chromosome from Meiosis I.

In Prophase I, the DNA tightly coils into chromosomes, spindle fibers appear, and the nucleus and nucleolus disassemble. The two copies of each chromosome (called chromatids) stay connected to each other by the centromere. Chromosomes line up next to their homologues (called synapsis) forming a tetrad. During synapsis, the chromatids within a homologous pair twist around one another (forming a chiasma), allowing portions of chromatids to break off and attach to adjacent chromatids on the homologous chromosome in a process called crossing-over. This exchange of genetic material between maternal and paternal chromosomes results in genetic recombination.

During Metaphase I, tetrads line up randomly along the midline of the dividing cell, the metaphase plate. Spindle fibers from one pole attach to the centromere of one homologous chromosome and spindle fibers from the other pole attach to the centromere of the other homologous chromosome of the pair. This looks similar to metaphase in mitosis, except that the spindle microtubules are only able to attach to kinetochore proteins on the outside of each centromere.

In Anaphase I, each homologous chromosome (consisting of two chromatids attached by a centromere) moves to an opposite pole of the dividing cell. Random separation of the homologous chromosomes is called independent assortment.

As Telophase I and Cytokinesis I progress, chromosomes reach the opposite ends of the cell and form a cluster at each pole. The nuclear membrane re-forms and the parent cell divides the organelles and cytoplasm between the two daughter cells. New cells contain a haploid number of chromosomes but two copies of each chromatid.

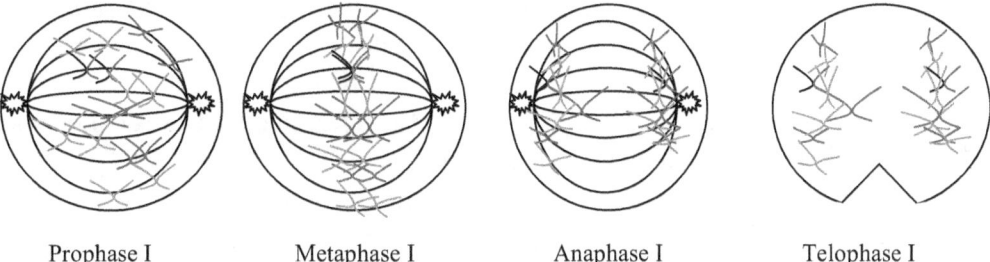

Prophase I   Metaphase I   Anaphase I   Telophase I

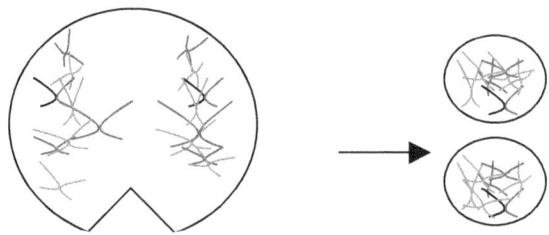

Cytokinesis I

After a brief interphase with no replication of DNA, prophase II starts. The spindle fibers form and begin to move the chromosomes toward the midline of the dividing cells.

In metaphase II, the chromosomes (consisting of sister chromatids) move to the midline of the dividing cell, facing opposite poles of the dividing cell. Kinetochore microtubules from opposite poles attach to opposite sides of the same centromere.

In anaphase II, the chromatids separate and move toward opposite poles of the cell.

During telophase II and cytokinesis II, the nuclear membrane forms around the cluster of chromosomes in each of the four new cells. After cytokinesis II, there are four new cells each containing half of original cell's number of chromosomes. No two cells are alike due to genetic recombination.

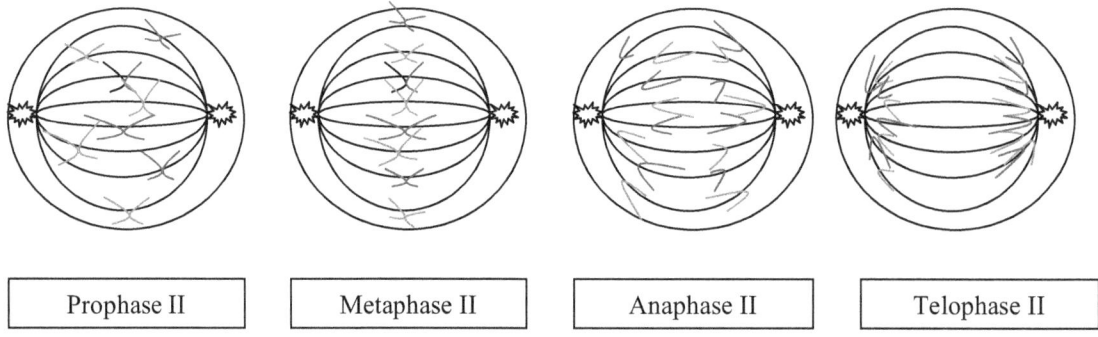

| Prophase II | Metaphase II | Anaphase II | Telophase II |

In animals, meiosis produces haploid reproductive cells called gametes. Meiosis only occurs in reproductive organs (testes in males and ovaries in female). Spermatogenesis is the production of four male gametes known as sperm cells in the testes. Each diploid reproductive cell divides meiotically to form four haploid cells called spermatids, each of which then develops into a mature sperm cell. Oogenesis is the name of the female's production of one mature egg cell or ovum. A diploid reproductive cell divides meiotically to produce one mature egg cell (ovum) and three polar bodies which degenerate (die). During cytokinesis I and cytokinesis II of oogenesis the cytoplasm of the original cell is divided unequally between new cells, giving the ovum the majority.

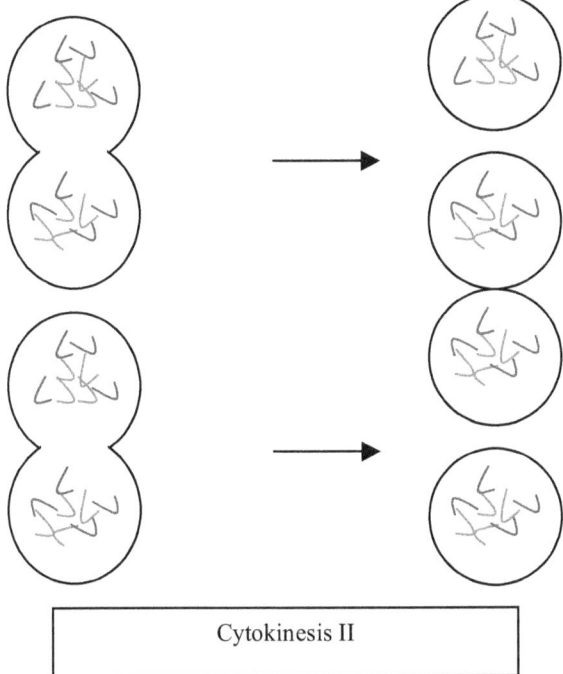

Cytokinesis II

Asexual reproduction is the production of offspring from one parent rather than from two parents and does not usually involve meiosis or the union of gametes. In unicellular organisms, such as bacteria, new organisms are created by either binary fission or mitosis. In multicellular organisms, asexual reproduction results from the budding off of portions of their bodies, so that each "offspring" is genetically identical to the one parent.

Sexual reproduction is the production of offspring through meiosis and the union of a sperm and an egg. Offspring produced by sexual reproduction are genetically different from the parents because genes are combined in new ways in meiosis. Except for identical twins, sexually produced offspring contain unique combinations of their parents' genes. This enables a species to adapt rapidly to new conditions.

MEIOSIS

Meiosis is the type of cell division that results in "germ cells," or eggs and sperm (also called gametes), and involves a reduction in the amount of genetic material rather than cloning it. It also produces not two daughter cells, but four, and involves two phases: first division and gamete formation.

In first division, the following phases occur:

Prophase 1. Each chromosome duplicates, but the parts remain close together. The duplicated chromosomes are called sister chromatoids. In this stage, it is possible for "crossing over," or DNA recombination to occur.

Metaphase 1. Homologous chromosomes align at the equatorial plate.

Anaphase 1. The homologous pairs separate while the sister chromatoids remain together.

Telophase 1. Two daughter cells are formed, with each containing only one chromosome from the homologous pair.

So, once there are two cells, the gametes form as the following phases occur:

Prophase 2. DNA does not replicate.

Metaphase 2. Chromosomes align at the equatorial plate.

Anaphase 2. The centromeres (the area where the spindle attaches) and sister chromatids migrate separately to each pole.

Telophase 2. Cell division is complete and four haploid daughter cells are created.

6. BASIC GENE STRUCTURE/CHEMICAL NATURE OF THE GENE

WATSON-CRICK MODEL OF NUCLEIC ACIDS

In 1953, James Watson and Francis Crick (Cambridge University) proposed that the structure of the DNA molecule was two chains of nucleotides that are intertwined to make a double helix. Each strand is made up of repeating sugar and phosphate units joined by phosphodiester bonds. The two strands are wrapped around a common axis similar to two strands of rope, held together with crossbars. A nucleotide is composed of a phosphate group, a deoxyribose group, and a nitrogen-containing base (either purine or pyrimidine). A DNA molecule can have as many as 200,000 nucleotides. The two strands are held together by weak hydrogen bonds between a purine and its opposing pyrimidine.

Because of the shapes of the purines and pyrimidines, and the fact that hydrogen bonds function only over short distances, adenine can pair only with thymine and guanine will pair only with cytosine. Therefore, the number of thymines in a particular kind of DNA will equal the number of adenines and likewise for guanines and cytosines. The nucleotides of a single strand may be linked together in any arrangement and each nucleotide can be repeated as often as desired. Once the order of one strand is established, it determines the order of the other strand. The total amount of DNA in similar kinds of cells remains constant from generation to generation, implying that both the quality and the quantity of the DNA remains the same in similar cells derived from the same parent cell.

DNA REPLICATION

The Watson-Crick model suggests that the copying of DNA is complementary since the order of one strand determines the order of the other strand. Replication is accomplished by "unzipping" the two strands of the helix. Each strand can then add nucleotides to itself in the correct complementary order, using various enzymes. After replication the two identical DNA's each contains one strand that is original and one that is new. The stages of replication are initiation, elongation, and termination.

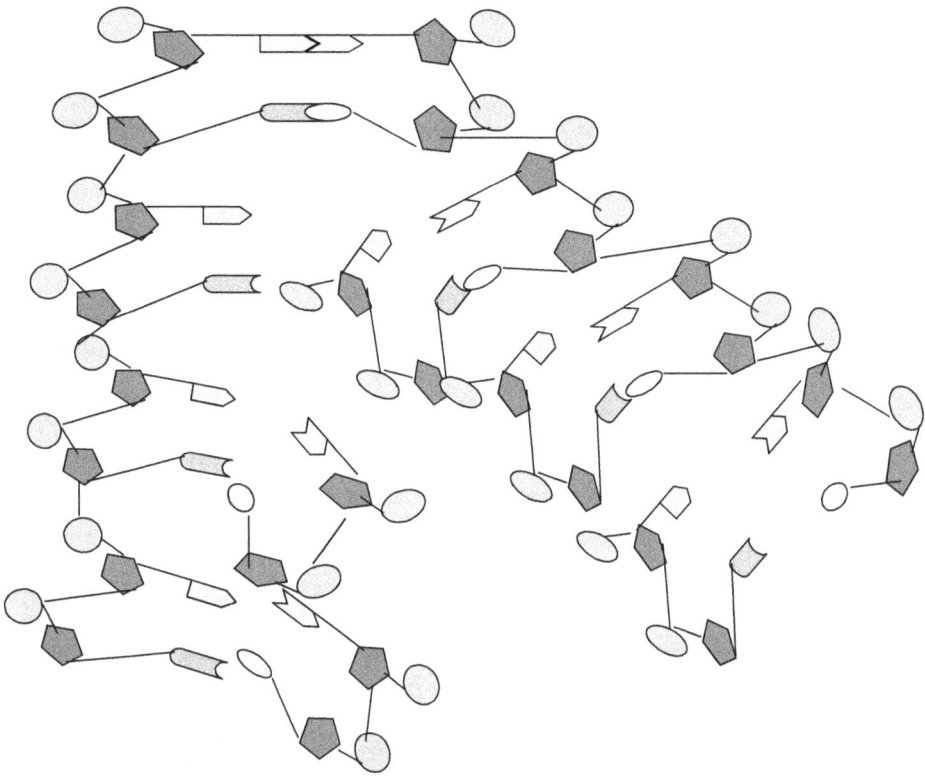

MUTATIONS

A mutation is a permanent change in a cell's DNA. It can be a change in nucleotide sequence, alteration of gene position, gene loss or duplication, or an insertion of one or several foreign sequence(s). One type of mutation at the chromosomal level is an inversion of genes where a specific section is reversed. Another type is translocation of genes where information from one of two homologous chromosomes breaks and binds to the other. This type is usually lethal. Alterations of DNA sequence include deletion, insertion, inversion and substitution. Negatively, mutations are the cause of many defects and diseases and can cause death. Positively, mutations increase genetic diversity and allow for a wider variation of traits for natural selection.

CONTROL OF PROTEIN SYNTHESIS: TRANSCRIPTION, TRANSLATION, POSTTRANSCRIPTIONAL PROCESSING

The information in genes is expressed in two steps. First it is transcribed into RNA using tRNA and rRNA. Ribosomal RNA (rRNA) provides the site during protein synthesis where polypeptides are assembled. Transfer RNA (tRNA) transports amino acids to the ribosome to be used in building the polypeptides and position each amino acid at the correct place. Messenger RNA (mRNA) molecules are long strands of RNA that are transcribed from DNA and travel to the ribosomes to direct precisely which amino acids are assembled into polypeptides. Each "word" or codon of three nucleotides in a specific sequence corresponds to one of the twenty amino acids.

STRUCTURAL AND REGULATORY GENES

DNA, the molecule responsible for the inheritance of traits, is divided into functional units called genes. Gene expression is controlled by regulating transcription either at the transcriptional or post-transcriptional levels. The most common method of control is at the transcriptional level. Regulatory proteins identify DNA sequences without unwinding the helix by inserting DNA-binding motifs into the major groove where the edges of the base-pairs are exposed.

In prokaryotic gene regulation, repressors are proteins that bind to regulatory sites on DNA and prevent or decrease initiation of transcription and activators are proteins that bind to regulatory sites on the DNA to stimulate the initiation of transcription.

Eukaryotic transcription factors include basal transcriptional factors and specific transcriptional factors, enhancers, coactivators, and mediators. Post-transcriptional control of gene expression is exercised by proteins and small RNAs. Proteins interacting with small RNA can carry out alternative splicing of RNA transcripts. Chemical alterations of specific bases cause TNA transcript editing. Translation repression and selective degradation of mRNA transcripts provide further control of gene expression.

TRANSFORMATION

Plant transformation is the stable introduction of a gene into a plant genome using a multifaceted protocol that requires a gene delivery system, and a reliable culturing system for regenerating plant tissue sections into mature plants.

Gene transformation is the process of introducing genes into plants by methods which bypass the sexual seed production process. Essentially, it is a process by which genes are "cut" from the cells of one organism and "pasted" and integrated into the cells of another organism. Once the cells are transformed, they are grown into new plants capable of "expressing" a desired characteristic. Genes that are resistant to specific diseases, antifungal, antibacterial, or resistant to toxicity are the most desirable to use for transformation.

VIRUSES

The viruses of eukaryotes are similar to prokaryote infecting viruses. Proviruses are viral DNA integrated into the host cell. Some of the DNA viruses can either initiate an infection (lytic in prokaryotes) cycle or can form proviruses. Simian Virus 40 (SV40) causes cancer in hamsters but not in its normal hosts. SV40 and a number of other viruses can introduce new functional genes into the host DNA.

Retroviruses can also insert their nucleic acid into host DNA via reverse transcriptase which is carried with the RNA into the host cell. The inserted viral DNA makes RNA transcripts which are packaged with viral protein coats and reverse transcriptase. The viral DNA may, depending on its insertion point, cause mutations of the host DNA. Most viral DNA insertions do not damage the host, but rather become part of the host genome and can be passed on if they have managed to infect a germ-line cell.

Cancer is a disease in which cells escape the restraints on normal cell growth. Cancer is an inheritable disease (at least from cell to daughter cells). Once a cell has become cancerous, all of its descendant cells are cancerous. Gross chromosomal abnormalities are often visible in cancerous cells. Most carcinogens (cancer generating factors) are also mutagens (mutation generating factors). Oncogenes are genes resembling normal genes but in which something has gone wrong, resulting in a cancer.

Viruses seem able to cause cancer in three ways. Presence of the viral DNA may disrupt normal host DNA functions. Viral proteins needed for virus replication may also affect normal host gene regulation. Since most cancer causing viruses are retroviruses, the virus may serve as a vector for oncogene insertion. Viruses can thus serve as a possible vector to place healthy (non-mutated) alleles into eggs.

To understand the structure of a gene, you must understand the molecules that make it up. DNA is a molecule that encodes genetic information. For most cells, it is a long coiled, double stranded chain of interlocking base pairs known as a double helix. DNA is made up of four bases: adenine (A), thymine (T), guanine (G), and cytosine (C). The sequence of these bases creates a code for information. So, if these bases are arranged in the formation ATC, the information contained within that sequence will be different than if the bases were arranged differently, such as in TCA. All living cells are equipped with the ability to read the sequence and act upon the encoded information. All the genetic information stored in the cells is referred to collectively as a genome. A single copy of a human genome is nearly three billion bases long.

A gene is but a section of the DNA strand. This section carries specific instructions for a specific function. While all humans have basically the same genes, there are a lot of different versions known as alleles. These alleles affect things such as eye color, hair color and more. So, it's the same gene – we all have eyes and hair – but the allele determines the color, making each human genetically unique.

All eukaryotic cells have chromosomes, which are strands of DNA bundled together by proteins. Humans happen to have 22 numbered chromosomes, plus the X and Y chromosomes that make us male or female. A typical cell will contain two copies each of the numbered chromosomes, one from each parent, and two sex chromosomes. The collection of an individual cell's chromosomes is known as a karyotype.

The function of genes is essentially to store information and tell our cells what to do – how to differentiate and carry out messages to other cells. However, since genetic information is located in the nucleus of every cell, how does it get out? Here are the steps cells go through to carry information to other cells:

Transcription. This is the first step in interpreting information stored in genes. During this process, copies of the information contained in the DNA are made. The resulting copy of the DNA is called a "messenger RNA" or "mRNA." RNA is similar to DNA in that it is also an information coding molecule; however, it is made up of just one strand and uses a different base, uracil (U), in the place of the thyamine (T) in DNA.

Translation. To make proteins in the cell, the mRNA attaches itself to the cell's ribosomes, which are capable of reading genetic information, and in turn create proteins, a process known as translation.

BIOENERGETICS AND BIOSYNTHESIS

Bioenergetics is a field of biology that studies the production of energy in life forms. In this section, we will look at bioenergetics as it relates to the life of a cell. We all know that cells need energy in order to maintain life. If a cell fails to transform energy, such as food, into a form it can use then that cell dies.

Cells get their energy from a variety of sources: ATP, respiration, the sun, and oxidation. ATP is an abbreviation for adenosine triphosphate and is present in all living cells. Its function is to carry energy across cell membranes. Through a process called respiration, which all cells use in some form, the energy stored in chemical bonds is liberated then recaptured in ATP molecules which in turn carry it around dispersing it as necessary. In order to bind energy in ATP molecules, two chemical reactions must take place. The first reaction is known as glycosis. In this process, glucose, or the energy from food, is broken down. The second reaction, known as the Krebs' cycle, which is where oxidation comes in, is a 10-step chemical reaction that occurs in the cell's mitochondria.

Another way that cells get energy is through solar power. Most plants, and many bacteria, practice photosynthesis, a process through which food is "created" for them by the sun, water and carbon dioxide.

Biosynthesis is the process through which the energy produced by all these methods is used. Essentially, cells use all the energy they obtain from these various sources as a means to procreate or produce more cells.

7. ORGANISM DEVELOPMENT, GENETICS, AND HEREDITY

This section will focus on the development of organisms as well as the basic concepts of heredity.

ORGANISM DEVELOPMENT

This section will discuss the development of multicellular organisms such as plants and animals. As discussed, all cells contain genetic data that determine what each cell will do. This data cause the cells of multicellular organisms to specialize, resulting in different cells for different functions.

The first cellular specialization occurred nearly a half-billion years ago, resulting in cells that could perform a function to the benefit of the entire multicellular organism as a whole. The difference between then and now was that, if removed from the host organism, these cells could still function independently. The great turning point was when multicellular organisms began to reproduce through sex, rather than through mitosis, creating new organisms that were no longer exact copies of their ancestors, but instead contained only 50 percent of the genetic information from their parents, allowing for a greater number of mutations and genetic variation, causing natural selection to take effect on the unique organisms.

The increased possibility for diversification through sexual reproduction resulted in more ecosystem niches being filled which in turn resulted in increased competition for resources. This competition for resources meant that in order to survive, multicellular organisms would have to adapt fast enough to their environments in order to "stand the test of time," resulting in even further diversification and the creation of distinct plants and animals.

GENETICS AND PATTERNS OF HEREDITY

A monk named Gregor Mendel (1822 – 1884) was lauded as the father of genetics and heredity, and was the first person to trace the characteristics of successive generations of a living thing. Through experiments with pea plants, Mendel described how traits were inherited and published his work in the short monograph, "Experiments with Plant Hybrids," which became one of the most enduring publications of natural science.

From these experiments, Mendel derived the basic laws of heredity: inherited factors do not combine, but are passed intact from one generation to the next, and each member of the parental generation passes only half of its heredity factors to each offspring with certain factors "dominant" over others. Different offspring of those same parents will receive different sets of inherited factors.

Gregor Mendel was the father of genetics and inheritance. He was a priest in charge of a garden who got interested in some of the plants. Pea pods are self-fertilizing. Three of four seeds were purple, one seed out of four was white. Each plant contained two genetic codes. The purple was dominant over white because it showed up more often. Look at the chart below to determine the chances of getting each kind of plant:

PP=Purple (Upper case means dominant, lower case means recessive)
pp=White

	Purple	White
Purple	PP	Pp
White	pP	pp

The inheritance of sex is determined by the x and the y chromosome. All chromosomes come in pairs. For use in the chart, females are XX and males are XY.

	X	X
X	XX	XX
Y	YX	YX

To get the values (YX), all you do is add the intersection of each row and column on the table. According to the table on the previous page (and biology) the chances of having either a boy or girl are 50%. The chart above is called a Punnett Square.

In order to understand a Punnett square (the tables above and below) is it important to first understand the significance of phenotypes and genotypes. A phenotype is the physical appearance of the gene. For example, eye color, hair color, and earlobe type are all phenotypes. Phenotypes are determined by genotypes, which are the basically the genetic appearance of the trait, or in other words, what alleles are present. Genotypes are expressed as a combination of two alleles. When making Punnett squares, a trait is assigned a letter. The alleles are represented by capital or lowercase letters. An allele represented by a capital letter represents a dominant trait while an allele represented with a lowercase letter represents a recessive trait. If a trait is dominant, it means that it exerts phenotypic control and masks the recessive trait.

A Punnett square is a diagram which displays all of the possible crosses between an egg and sperm cell. Punnett squares are used to show the possible results of a simple genetic cross. The diagram below models the Punnett square of a cross between two Tt genotypes.

	T	T
T	TT	Tt
t	Tt	Tt

The Punnett square shows that TT and Tt and tt are the three possible results of the cross. The genotype TT contains two dominant alleles. This genotype is described as homozygous dominant. Homozygous means that the two alleles are the same, and because they are both dominant, the dominant phenotype appears. The table displays two Tt genotypes. This genotype is described as heterozygous, because the two alleles are not the same. In the case of a heterozygous result, the dominant phenotype manifests. The final possible result is a tt genotype.

This genotype is described has homozygous recessive. This is the only case in which the recessive trait will manifest. Any simple cross between two heterozygous genotypes will result in a 1 homozygous dominant: 2 heterozygous: 1 homozygous recessive ratio among the inheritance possibilities.

One example of a simple genetic cross in which this type of Punnett square is used is gender. In humans, gender is determined using X and Y alleles. The X allele contains a wide variety of genetic information, including female genetic information. It is recessive. The Y allele contains information relating to male genetic information and is dominant. The Punnett square below shows the possibility that emerges for each human child.

An XX genotype will result in a female child, and a XY genotype will result in a male child. As is shown above, the possibility of child being male or female is fifty percent.

This method works well for very simple genetic crosses, however most genetic traits are influenced by a number of genes. It is possible to construct a Punnett square which displays the possible crosses of multiple genes. A dihybrid cross, for example, is the cross between two homozygous dominant genes, such as AABB, and two homozygous recessive genes, such as aabb. However, the more genes are added, the more complex the system becomes. First it must be determined all of the possible matches between the two types of genes, and then all of those possibilities must be crossed. The Punnett square below demonstrates the cross between an AABB genotype and an AaBb genotype.

		AABB			
		AB	Ab	AB	Ab
AaBb	AB	AABB	AABb	AABB	AABb
	AB	AABB	AABb	AABB	AABb
	aB	AaBB	AaBb	AaBB	AaBb
	aB	AaBB	AaBb	AaBB	AaBb

Chromosomes in DNA carry genes.

Somatic Cell is a full set of chromosomes (there is a total of 46 chromosomes, thus 46 genes). Cloning is done by doing reproduction just using the somatic cell.

Gametes are the reproductive cells (eggs and sperm). Each has exactly one-half a set of normal chromosomes; this is why you need one of each to conceive. Gametes fuse together to make a zygote. A zygote is the first part of a human. Only a few genes are on the "y" chromosome. All genes on the "y" are passed on to boys every time, but never to girls.

There are some genes that are linked to the sex or gender of the person. **Hemophilia** is passed from mother to son, harmless to the mother but can be fatal to the son. Other disorders that can be passed are **colorblindness** and **muscular dystrophy**.

Animal Breeding

Pure bred dogs are dogs that are only bred with their same type of dog for a favorable trait or look. This can cause health problems for the dogs as sometimes the owners are inbreeding the animals. For example, this is responsible for Saint Bernards having poor hip bones. There are laws against human inbreeding for that same reason, because it can cause major health problems and deformations.

Polygenetic: two pairs of genes are used to determine what is passed on.

Rh Factor

Rh factor has to do with your blood. If you are A positive, you are Rh positive. If a husband and wife have different blood types, then it can cause a problem for the baby. If the baby has Rh positive blood and the mother is Rh negative it could cause the mother's cells to attack the baby. To fix this, injections are given in the doctor's office or hospital.

Albinism

From the National Organization of Albinism and Hyperpigmentation, here is some information about the disease: "People with albinism have little or no pigment in their eyes, skin, or hair. They have inherited genes that do not make the usual amounts of a pigment called melanin. When both parents carry the gene, and neither parent has albinism, there is a one in four chance at each pregnancy that the baby will be born with albinism. This type of inheritance is called autosomal recessive inheritance."[1] People who have it are sometimes called Albinos. Albinism can affect people from all races.

POPULATION BIOLOGY: THE STRUGGLE FOR EXISTENCE

The first studies on population ecology and biology were completed by Thomas Malthus, a British clergyman. In 1798, he published his work, "Essay on the Principle of Population," which asserted that at some point, the expanding population of any given species (including humans) will exceed its supply of natural resources, resulting in stronger competition for things like food, shelter, and other essentials.

This theory was expanded upon by none other than Charles Darwin, who included a section on population biology in his "On the Origin of Species."

In 1935, Harry Smith, a biological control worker at the University of California, established the terms we still use today to describe the competition for resources, "density-dependent" and "density-independent." Both these terms refer to mortality factors of any given species. A density dependent mortality factor is one that causes a varying degree of mortality in subject population. In other words, the mortality of a population is directly dependent upon the population's density. This serves as a biological control as once resources run out, members of a dense population begin to die, taking that population down to a number that can be sustained on the resources available.

Conversely, a density independent population, or one that continues to grow despite the presence of large numbers of members of that same competing species (like humans), does not result in the mortality of its members due to resource depletion. Instead, that population continues to grow denser despite the population growth and increased competition for resources.

Chemical/Physical Sciences

1. ATOMIC AND NUCLEAR STRUCTURE

In the last section of this study guide, we discussed that cells are what make up organisms, whether they are multicellular or single cell organisms. In this section, we will study things on an even smaller scale.

Molecules are the building blocks of any living cell. In fact, they are even more all encompassing, and are the building blocks of any matter, living or not. Molecules are defined by science as the "smallest portion of a pure element or compound that retains a set of unique chemical and physical properties." Cells are made up of macromolecules, or very large molecules, which consist of smaller molecules. Molecules are not considered to be living.

Molecules are made up of atoms, which make chemical compounds, which are the basis for everything in the universe both living and not living. All atoms consist of particles called electrons, protons, and neutrons. Each of these particles has different properties. Electrons are very small, light particles with a negative electric charge that orbit the nucleus of the atom. Protons are much heavier and have a positive charge, and are located inside the nucleus of an atom, along with the atom's neutrons. As the name would imply, neutrons have no electric charge. Like protons, they are very heavy. They are also quite large, relatively speaking. All atoms are made up of a combination of these particles.

Although they are relatively small, the nucleus of all atoms makes up the majority of an atom's mass. However, the electrons surrounding the nucleus make up the majority of an atom's volume. The area where electrons orbit the nucleus is referred to as the electron cloud and is subdivided into energy levels, or shells. Some very important atomic terms are as follows:

Atomic number. In the periodic table of elements, the atomic number is always representative of the number of protons contained in the nucleus of an atom.

Periodic Table of Elements. The periodic table of elements is a classification system developed by a man named Mendeleev based upon the chemical properties of elements.

Mass Number. The mass number of any atom is the number of protons plus the number of neutrons present in the nucleus of an atom. In other words, mass number equals the total number of particles present in the nucleus.

Element. Elements are atoms that all have the same atomic number.

Isotope. An isotope is an atom with the same atomic number as an element, but a different mass number.

Although they are often separated by the electron cloud, two or more nuclei can come into contact and interact with each other through the strong nuclear force, resulting in a reaction. Nuclear reactions, like all chemical reactions, can be either exothermic, resulting in a release of energy, or endothermic, requiring additional energy to occur. The two primary reactions nuclei engage in are fusion and fission:

Fusion. In fusion, two light nuclei (with a relatively small atomic mass) combine to form a single, heavier nucleus. A good example of this is thermonuclear weapons. Most thermonuclear weapons employ fusion, crashing two different hydrogen isotopes together in order to form helium. This results in a large output of energy in the form of an explosion, which can be devastating. In fact, thermonuclear reactions often occur in the formation of stars. Hydrogen isotopes will collide to form helium atoms, which will in turn collide to form yet heavier atoms. This basic reaction is what drives our sun.

Fission. The other type of reaction, fission, is a nuclear reaction that results in the splitting of a heavier nucleus into two lighter nuclei. An example of fission can be found in the first atomic bomb. As with fusion, great amounts of energy can be released from the reaction. Fission occurs because of the electrostatic repulsion created by the large number of positively charged protons contained in a heavy nucleus. These protons will push away from each other until they split in a burst of energy, resulting in two smaller nuclei with less electrostatic repulsion. Fission is used in a variety of ways, such as in energy production at nuclear power plants.

Isotopes are called radioisotopes when they have unstable nuclei that are radioactive. **Alpha particles** (α) are positively charged particles (+2) emitted from a radioactive nucleus. They consist of two protons and two neutrons and are identical to the nucleus of a helium atom ($^4_2 He$).

Example: $^{238}_{92} U \rightarrow ^4_2 He + ^{234}_{90} Th$.

When an atom loses an alpha particle, the Z number (atomic number) is lowered by two, so move back two spaces on the periodic table to find what the new element is. The new element has an A number (atomic mass number) that is four less than the original element. Because alpha particles are large and heavy, paper or clothing or even dead skin cells shield from their effects.

There are a number of different types of radioactive decay, the three most common of which are alpha decay, beta decay and gamma decay. When alpha decay occurs, the nucleus spontaneously (i.e. randomly or unpredictably) ejects what is essentially a helium nucleus, or a package of two protons and two neutrons. This results in the atomic number of the atom dropping by two, and the atomic mass dropping by four. Beta decay occurs when the number of neutrons is too high relative to the number of protons. Because the nuclear strong force will not allow an entire neutron to be ejected, the nucleus finds a different solution. When beta decay occurs a neutron is split into a positive and negative portion, becoming a proton and an electron, and the negative portion (i.e., the electron) is ejected. This results in the atomic mass remaining constant, the atomic number increasing by 1 and the charge decreasing by 1. The final type of radiation, gamma radiation, often occurs with other types of radiation when the electrons are left in too high of energy states (or in higher shells than they need to be). The electrons will jump down to the proper shells and emit a gamma ray, which is now known to be a photon (essentially, it just lets out a burst of energy in the form of light).

Beta rays (β) are negatively charged (-1) and fast moving because they are actually electrons. They are written as an electron $^0_{-1} e$ (along with a proton) which is emitted from the nucleus as a neutron decays. Carbon-14 decays by emitting a beta particle.

Example: $^{14}_6 C \rightarrow ^{14}_7 N + ^0_{-1} e$.

The Z number actually adds one since its total must be the same on both the left and the right of the arrow and the electron on the right adds a negative one. The A number is unchanged. The Z determines what the element is, so look for it on the periodic table to determine the product. Metal foil or wood is needed to shield from its effects.

Gamma rays (γ) are high energy electromagnetic waves. They are the same kind of radiation as visible light but of much shorter wavelength and higher frequency. Gamma rays have no mass or charge, so the Z and A numbers are not affected. Radioactive atoms often emit gamma rays along with either alpha or beta particles. Protection from gamma radiation takes lead or concrete.

Example 1: $^{226}_{88}Ra \rightarrow {}^{222}_{86}Rn + {}^{4}_{2}He + \gamma$

Example 2: $^{234}_{90}Th \rightarrow {}^{234}_{91}Pa + {}^{0}_{-1}e + \gamma$

A **positron** is a particle with the mass of an electron but a positive charge ($0 +1 e$). It may be emitted as a proton changes to a neutron.

Transmutation is the conversion of an atom of one element to an atom of another element such as occurs in alpha and beta radiation. It also occurs when high energy particles (such as protons, neutrons, or alpha particles) bombard the nucleus of an atom.

The elements in the periodic table with atomic numbers above 92 are called the trans uranium elements, all of which are radioactive elements that have been synthesized in nuclear reactors and nuclear accelerators.

Example: $^{238}_{92}U + {}^{1}_{0}n \rightarrow {}^{239}_{92}U \rightarrow {}^{0}_{-1}e + {}^{239}_{93}Np \rightarrow {}^{239}_{94}Pu + {}^{0}_{-1}e$

Nuclear fission is the splitting of a nucleus into smaller fragments by bombardment with neutrons. Fission releases enormous amounts of energy. Controlled fission is the source of the energy in nuclear power plants. In **nuclear fusion**, hydrogen nuclei fuse to make helium nuclei. Fusion releases even more energy than fission.

Every radioisotope has its own characteristic rate of decay. The **half-life of an isotope** is the time it takes for half the original amount of the isotope in a given sample to decay. For example, the half-life of carbon-14 is 5700 years. If there are 25 grams of carbon-14 in a petrified log, then 5700 years later it will contain 12.5 grams of carbon-14. Another 5700 years later it will contain 6.25 grams of C-14.

2. ELEMENTS, COMPOUNDS, REACTIONS, AND ATOMIC BONDS

All matter, living and non-living, is made up of elements. Elements, consisting of atoms, are defined as substances that cannot be decomposed into simpler substances by a chemical reaction.

On the periodic table of elements, each element is represented by one or more letters. To the left and right of these letters appear the atomic mass number, atomic number and number of neutrons.

A compound is a mixture of atoms of two or more different elements that have been chemically bonded. Atoms can bond in one of two ways: ionically or covalently. An ionic bond is an intramolecular force that is formed when electrons are transferred from one atom to another, creating ions that are electrostatically attracted to one another. A good example of an ionic bond is the formation of table salt. With table salt, which is a combination of sodium and chloride, the sodium gives up one of its electrons to chlorine. To start with, the sodium atom is negatively charged while the chloride atom is positively charged. In other words, the sodium atom has more electrons in its outer shell, while the chloride has few electrons in its outer shell. When the two bond, the electric charge in each is neutralized, forming a stable salt molecule.

A covalent bond is a chemical bond in which electrons are shared between atoms. A good example of covalent bonds at work is in the formation of a diamond. The carbon atoms that make up the diamond share electrons because their outer energy shells are only partially filled. All the atoms need the energy from the other atoms' electrons to be more stable. Therefore, the carbon molecules in a diamond form a vast network of covalent bonds, making diamond molecules some of the hardest on earth.

Chemical changes, or changes in the composition of chemicals, occur when there is a chemical reaction. There are several types of chemical reactions you should be aware of:

Combination or Synthesis Reaction. This reaction is the result of two or more substances uniting to create a compound.

Decomposition. Decomposition is a chemical reaction where a compound breaks down into two or more simpler substances.

Single Replacement. This type of reaction results when one element replaces another in a compound.

Double Replacement. A double replacement reaction is a reaction between two compounds in which elements or ions replace one another.

3. THERMODYNAMICS, STATES OF MATTER, CLASSICAL MECHANICS AND RELATIVITY

This section will discuss the laws of thermodynamics and how they affect the state of matter. This section will also delve into classical mechanics and relativity.

THERMODYNAMICS

To understand thermodynamics, it is important to realize that the term "system" is applied to whatever it is that is being studied. This might seem somewhat obvious; however, thermodynamics can be very specific so you have to know exactly what you are studying. A system can be microscopic or very large. For example, a biochemist studying the effect of toxins on humans might define their system as a single human cell, while an atmospheric chemist might look at the chemical composition of the atmosphere of the entire earth.

Energy in thermodynamics is the ability to do work or produce heat. The kinetic energy of a system is the energy of motion, or the energy produced by the motion of molecules and the electrons within the atoms. Potential energy is considered stored energy, and can result from the position or configuration of a given system. Chemical potential energy is stored in the bonds of its compounds and when a chemical reaction occurs, atoms are rearranged, and the reconfiguration of the atoms causes energy to change. The total of the kinetic and potential energy of all particles within a chemical system is referred to as "internal energy."

Some other important things to know when studying thermodynamics are the definitions of "work" and "heat."

Work. Work is equal to force times distance, or in chemistry, the force applied to something during a chemical reaction. A good example of this in motion is this: say you have a bottle full of water to which you add alka-seltzer, then you put a stopper on the bottle. The resultant chemical reaction generates a gas, which expands in the container and forces the stopper out. The external pressure outside the container, or the pressure keeping the stopper in, will be assumed to be at one atmosphere. The work done during the chemical reaction is equal to the external pressure multiplied by the change in the volume. This is also called "PV work," and that is what chemical work refers to.

Heat. Heat is the transfer of energy from a body of higher temperature to a body of lower temperature. So, heat involves the flow of energy from one body to another. In studying thermodynamics, the primary concern is the flow of heat to a system's surroundings. The most common units to express heat are the joule and the calorie.

There are two laws of thermodynamics that are absolutely vital in chemistry:

Law 1. Energy can be neither created nor destroyed. In other words, there is a certain amount of energy present in the universe, and it can be converted from one form to another, but you cannot increase the amount of energy in the universe or decrease it. The second part of the first law is that the change in internal energy of any system is equal to heat plus work.

Law 2. While there is a finite amount of energy in the universe, its quality is degraded irreversibly. In other words, every time a chemical reaction takes place, or every time energy is expended to cause something to happen, part of the energy required to do the work is transformed into some other form than that which helped to perform the work. The most common method used to explain this second law is that all systems free of external influences become more disordered with time, which can be expressed in terms of the quantity called entropy.

STATES OF MATTER

As we know, matter is everywhere. You can't get away from it. It is anything that has mass and takes up space, no matter how light that mass is or how small the space is that it takes up.

Matter has both physical and chemical properties. Physical properties include the density of matter, melting points, boiling points, freezing points, or even color or smell. The most important chemical property that defines matter is the way elements combine in reactions. Matter can change in two major ways: physically and chemically. Matter exists in four primary phases or states: solids, liquids, gases, and plasmas. Elements and compounds can move from one phase to another when physical forces are present. The physical forces cause the matter's atoms to rearrange themselves resulting in a change of state.

One of these forces is temperature. When the temperature of a system changes, the phase of the matter involved often changes. In general, when the temperature of a compound or element rises, matter moves to a more "active" state. A compound or element can move from one phase to another and still be the same substance. For example, when you boil a pot of water, you can see water vapor hovering over it. Within the vapor, the atoms are less structured than they would be had the water been in liquid or solid form. The vapor can condense and become a drop of water which if put in the freezer would become solid.

If you introduce a chemical change to matter that would change the way that matter acted and eventually, the matter would become something else. For example, if you took a glass of water and added a new chemical to it, although the resulting substance might still be liquid, it would probably have slightly different properties. If you added alka-seltzer to a glass of water, the liquid would become fizzy and filled with bubbles and would release a gas.

Each state of matter has its own physical properties. Take a liquid, for example. Any given liquid will take the shape of the container holding it. It is very difficult to compress into a smaller space. In fact, it is very difficult to compress either a solid or a liquid into a smaller space, as when you compress something; you apply pressure to it in order to put the atoms together. In a liquid and a solid, the atoms are already fairly close, so it's difficult to get them closer. That is not the case with plasmas and gases.

CLASSICAL MECHANICS

The mechanics side of chemistry deals with the calculation and analysis of energies and spatial distributions of small particles (often the electrons of an atom or molecule) confined to small regions of space (usually limited to the perimeter of an atom or molecule). This is one of the many areas where chemistry and physics overlap.

About 70 years ago, it was commonly accepted that electrons orbited the nucleus of an atom, which is true. However, they don't orbit the nucleus like a planet orbits the sun. If electrons behaved that way, they would spiral in and crash into the nucleus within about a half a second. Instead, electrons orbit the nucleus in different energy shells.

However, it is impossible to know exactly where any given electron is at any particular time. Science has proven that it is impossible to know exactly where something is at any given time on an atomic scale. For example, if you wanted to find out where an electron was, just looking at an electron depends largely upon light. After all, you can't see the electron without light. Light is made of photons, which could develop enough momentum that once they come into contact with the electron, they might change its course. So, by the very act of looking at the electron, you might affect it.

A scientist by the name of Werner Heisenberg was the first to realize that there is an inherent uncertainty when trying to establish certain pairs of measurements, particularly on the atomic level. He was the father of the Heisenberg Uncertainty Principle, which states that you cannot know the exact location and velocity of a moving object at the same time. In fact, Heisenberg recognized that the more accurate you measure an electron's location, the less accurate a measurement of its velocity is, and vice versa.

Now, no discussion of quantum mechanics would be complete without a description of Schrödinger's equation. This differential equation, developed by Erwin Schrödinger in 1925, illustrates how all particles (electrons included) are characterized by a wave function. Unfortunately for scientists, it is impossible to determine an exact solution to the equation, so several assumptions are used in order to arrive at an approximate answer for any particular problem. The only time the equation can actually be solved is when there is no force acting upon the particle in question and its potential energy is zero.

RELATIVITY

Relativity is essential to quantum mechanics. Albert Einstein, the father of relativity, gave us both special relativity and general relativity. In his law of special relativity, he demonstrated that neither distance nor time is absolute and both can be affected by the motion of the observer. General relativity explained that time and space were affected by gravity.

In particular, the gravity of any given mass, such as our sun, can warp space and time around it. On an atomic level, the mass of the nucleus of the atom can affect the rotation of electrons around it.

4. ELECTRICITY AND MAGNETISM, LIGHT AND SOUND

In this section, we will discuss how atoms produce electricity, how magnetism works, and how light and sound travel.

ELECTRICITY

Electricity as we know it (i.e., the electricity that powers lights, televisions, and other electronic gadgets) is caused by the flow of electrons between atoms. As one electron attaches itself to an atom, that same atom loses an electron, which attaches itself to another atom, and so on, creating a current of electricity.

Certain atoms conduct electricity better than others. While some atoms hold their electrons very tightly, others hold them more loosely. When electrons are held very tightly to an atom, they do not move as freely as those held more loosely, so electricity cannot be conducted very well through materials made up of those atoms. Materials made of atoms that hold their electrons tightly are known as insulators. Good examples of insulators are rubber, plastic, cloth, glass, and dry air. Materials with atoms that hold their electrons loosely are known as conductors. Good examples of conductors include most metals (copper, aluminum or steel).

Another form of electrical energy is static electricity. Unlike the electricity that flows in a current, static electricity remains in one place. Some very common examples of static electricity include lightning and electric shocks, which often occur when shuffling your feet across a carpet.

No discussion of electricity would be complete without mentioning Benjamin Franklin, and the slightly less well known William Watson. In 1747, Franklin, in America, and Watson, in England, both did quite a bit of experimenting with electricity. They reached the same conclusion, that all materials are possessed of a kind of electrical "fluid." They surmised that the fluid, which couldn't be created or destroyed, moved from one object to another by the action of rubbing, electrifying both objects. Franklin theorized that the presence of the fluid created a positive charge, while lack of it caused negative charge, and that the direction of the flow of the fluid would always be from positive to negative, which is the opposite of what is actually true, as we now know that electrons will always seek out protons, not vice versa. However, these theories were definitely a step in the right direction, and set the tone for future scientific experiments on electricity.

MAGNETISM

The simplest way to describe magnetism is by saying that it is a force between two parallel electric currents. Those currents pointing in the same direction will attract each other, while those pointing in opposite directions will repel each other. The earliest known magnet was that produced by iron.

It was not until 1821 that a different type of magnet was discovered by a Danish scientist, Hans Christian Oersted, who noticed that the current flowing through a wire caused a nearby compass needle to move. This phenomenon was studied in France by Andre Marie Ampere, who came up with today's definition of magnetism, indicating that most magnets were, as stated earlier, a result of the force between two electric currents.

To visualize this force, or magnetic field, scientist Michael Faraday proposed a method that is widely used today. Picture a compass needle suspended freely in three dimensions close to a magnet or electric current. When you follow the direction of the needle it is possible to trace in space the lines obtained. These lines are called "field lines" and can also be illustrated in two dimensions using a bar magnet by sprinkling iron fillings on a sheet of paper held over a magnet. Those fillings will all cluster around the ends of the magnet.

To chemical scientists, field lines are a helpful method of displaying the structure of magnetic force. However, in astronomy, they are incredibly useful. Electrons and ions tend to stay attached to these field lines, sort of like beads on a wire, occasionally becoming trapped on the lines in the right conditions. When this happens, they define the direction of gas in space (which is hard to come by since space is a vacuum). That way astronomers and space researchers can study which way gas moves in the vacuum of space.

The scientist Faraday also discovered that the space around a magnet was filled not only with field lines, but was also modified by the magnetism. A Scottish physicist, James Clerk Maxwell, proved this theory mathematically, concluding that the modified space around a magnet was an electromagnetic field.

These fields can undergo wave motion, spreading with the speed of light. In fact, Maxwell discovered that this field was light in the form of an electromagnetic wave being modified by the magnet exerting force upon the field.

LIGHT

In the 1600s, Sir Isaac Newton determined that light was made up of particles while Thomas Young studied light in 1803 and determined that light was a wave in motion. While Newton's theory of light explained the straight-line casting of sharp shadows of objects placed in a strong light beam, it did not explain why shadows become less sharp with the interference of light.

Experiments with electromagnetism by the Scottish scientist Maxwell determined that light is electromagnetic in nature, beginning as a wave from the source of the light to the receiver. So, by the end of the 1800s, it seemed that light was indeed a wave rather than particles. However, with the discovery of X-rays, or electromagnetic waves with a short wavelength, in 1895 by Wilhelm Conrad Röntgen, the theory was questioned yet again. Another scientist studying X-rays, Arthur H. Compton, noted that X-rays act just like light, leading to even further scrutiny of the nature of light. It was not until 1921 that Albert Einstein realized that light sometimes acts as particles and sometimes acts like a wave. This would explain why, when light was shined upon metal, metal released electrons. It was because the metal was being bombarded by particles causing it to release energy.

The dual nature of light was not officially accepted by the scientific community until nearly the middle of the 20th century.

A few important definitions when discussing the measurement of light are as follows:

Photon. Photons are particles communicating force between charged particles. They are what allow for the interaction of particles with one another in an electromagnetic field. Completely massless, the photon is primarily associated with visible light. An important thing to know about photons is that they are affected by gravitational forces.

Speed of Light. The speed of light is the speed with which one photon travels through time and space. In a vacuum, a photon will travel 3×10^8 m/s-1.

Electromagnetic Radiation. This radiation is a combination of oscillating electric and magnetic fields. They are normally perpendicular to each other through space and carry energy from one place to another. Light is one form of electromagnetic radiation.

SOUND

Sound is known as a longitudinal, mechanical wave capable of traveling through any medium but a vacuum. So, there is no sound in outer space. Sound is produced by a variation in pressure. Increased pressure on a sound wave is called a compression, while decreased pressure on a sound wave is called a rarefaction, or dilation.

The speed with which sound travels is completely dependent upon the medium through which it is traveling and the state of the sound wave. Sound also comes in different frequencies. A high frequency sound is said to be "high pitched," while a low frequency sound is said to be "low pitched." Those sounds with a frequency above the range of human hearing are called ultrasound, and those with frequencies below the range of human hearing are known as infrasound.

Sound travels at a finite speed and can bend around corners, much like water waves. There is little controversy surrounding the idea of sound as a wave.

5. THE UNIVERSE, GALAXIES, SOLAR SYSTEMS, AND STARS

The nature of the universe, like evolution, has been hotly debated since the beginning of written history. Creationists hold that the universe was created approximately 6,000 years ago, while scientists hold that it was created billions of years ago. Both sides dissent not only on the time of creation, but also on the method of creation. In this section, we will discuss the creation of the universe, as well as the nature of galaxies, solar systems, and stars.

THE UNIVERSE

How the universe began, or even if it did indeed have a beginning is a great, great mystery and one that may never be completely solved. However, the prevalent theory of today is that our universe began as a single point of infinitesimal size and infinite mass. That point gave rise to what is known as the Big Bang, an incredible explosion that caused the universe to begin to expand. This expansion continues today.

The age of our universe is probably almost 12 billion years. Some theories set this age as even older – around 15 to 18 billion years.

Although it would seem that we really have no way of knowing how our universe started or how old it is, we have been able to positively determine from the observations of 20th century scientist Edwin Hubble that the universe is indeed expanding. This tells us that there would have to have been a point at some time from which this expansion began. The expansion of this point would have to have been powered by an unimaginably large energy surge in order to cause the universe to expand at the rate we currently observe. So, how do we know that this information is correct and that the Big Bang really did occur?

Well, the most compelling evidence for the Big Bang can be found in cosmic radiation. Discovered in 1965 by Arno Penzias and Robert Wilson, cosmic radiation is a uniform radiation throughout every region in space. Because the Big Bang would have occurred everywhere in the universe, the radiation should fill the space uniformly, and it does. Cosmic radiation also tells us that, at its inception, the universe was a very homogeneous place.

GALAXIES

Galaxies are huge collections of anywhere from millions to trillions of stars, gas, and dust, that are all held together by the gravitational attraction of their components. Galaxies rotate, which prevents them from collapsing in on themselves. Galaxies can be anywhere from several thousand to hundreds of thousands of light years across (a light year is the distance light travels in a year, or 5,880,000,000,000 miles).

Scientists at NASA hypothesize that galaxies began forming when the universe was a few hundred million years old. The first galaxies were probably just clusters of a few million stars. However, as the galaxies processed the chemicals resulting from the Big Bang, they grew more and more complex. Today's universe contains two primary types of galaxies: spirals and ellipticals. There are also irregularly shaped galaxies, which are not quite as common as spirals and ellipticals.

Spiral Galaxies. Spiral galaxies are similar to the Milky Way where our Earth resides. They have a bulge and a disk where stars form and two or more arms winding out from the central disk.

Elliptical Galaxies. Elliptical galaxies are much more common than spiral galaxies and usually do not have a disk in the center. That means that no new stars are forming.

Irregular Galaxies. Irregular galaxies come in many shapes and sizes. They are basically any galaxies that are neither spiral nor elliptical. They have been distorted by the gravitational pull of neighboring galaxies, which makes the irregular galaxy display strange shapes and lose its definite structure, if it ever had one.

SOLAR SYSTEMS

Most solar systems contain a family of planets orbiting around a large star, like our sun. In this section, we'll discuss the formation of solar systems, using our solar system as a model.

Starting from the position of the sun, the planets fall in this order:

- Mercury
- Venus
- Earth
- Mars - the most similar planet to Earth
- Jupiter - has the most mass of any planet in our solar system (including Earth)
- Saturn
- Uranus
- Neptune

NEBULAR HYPOTHESIS

The currently accepted hypothesis for the formation of Earth's solar system is called the Nebular Hypothesis. This theory was actually proposed by Immanual Kant and Pierre Simone Laplace in the 18th century. The Nebular Hypothesis states that a large cloud of dust in our galaxy called a nebula began to collapse from the pressure of the gravitational forces exerted upon it. The nebula was probably spinning slowly, but picked up speed as it began to contract in upon itself. The rotation and gravity gradually caused the nebula to flatten, much like a spinning pancake with a bulge in the center.

As the nebula continued to collapse, certain instabilities in the cloud caused local regions to contract gravitationally called condensation. These areas of condensation would later become the sun, planets, moons and other solar system debris.

STARS

Discussion of the formation of solar systems leads us to the formation of stars. Stars are actually huge balls of hydrogen gas that are being compressed until the temperatures and pressures in their cores increase until they burn hydrogen, which produces a lot of energy. This process, as we discussed earlier, is called fusion, or the compression of smaller, lighter atomic nuclei until they form larger, heavier nuclei, producing a large amount of energy as a byproduct. The element produced by this fusion is helium.

So, in order to form stars there must be hydrogen and there must be pressure, and lots of it. Although hydrogen is the most common chemical in the universe, there is only one atom of hydrogen per cubic centimeter. Hydrogen is often present in "molecular clouds" that contain hydrogen at a somewhat low temperature. To form a star, something needs to happen that will compress one of these molecular clouds to the point where it starts to collapse under its own gravity.

The process of star formation, or the formation of "protostars," can be set in motion by a variety of triggers: a passing star exerting pressure on the molecular cloud or the shock wave of a distant supernova (exploding star). Whatever the trigger, when the cloud begins to compress, hydrogen molecules get active. They begin colliding with each other, but are still pulled together by gravity which also causes more material to be dragged into the cloud around them. This disturbance will make the ball of gas rotate, and that rotation will speed up as more material is dragged in. As the star picks up speed, material begins to be flung out at the forming star's poles, flattening the new star into a disk around its middle or equator. As the cloud continues to collapse, the hydrogen molecules are pushed closer and closer together. Every time they collide, they generate heat, which raises the temperature of the forming star. Finally, the temperature is so high that the molecules of hydrogen will split into atoms. All the while, the rotation of the protostar is dragging in more material and more hydrogen. The core of the protostar becomes hotter and denser until it finally reaches a temperature of about 10 million degrees. At this temperature, the star can begin nuclear reactions that burn hydrogen and release energy. So, now the protostar has become a star and energy being forced out of it causes an outward pressure that balances and stops the star from collapsing inward completely. At last, the energy generated by the star bursts out of the upper layers of the star as light, which makes the star shine.

6. THE EARTH

In this section, we will look at many different parts of our planet, including our atmosphere, hydrosphere, the structure of the Earth, and a few other things.

EARTH'S ATMOSPHERE

Earth's atmosphere is comprised of four distinct layers:

Troposphere. The layer closest to Earth, this is where all of Earth's weather takes place.

Stratosphere and Ozone Layer. Just above the troposphere is the stratosphere. In this area, the direction of the wind is basically horizontal. Just over the stratosphere is the ozone layer, a relatively thin layer that protects the Earth from extremely intense, harmful ultraviolet rays from the sun.

Mesosphere. The mesosphere is just above the ozone layer and just below the ionosphere.

Ionosphere. This region is very ionized, hence its name. The ionosphere is very thin, and this is the area where the aurora borealis, or northern lights, occur. This layer of the atmosphere is also where the strongest of the sun's photons are deflected, and radio waves are reflected, which makes radio communication possible.

HYDROSPHERE

The Earth's hydrosphere encompasses all the water on Earth including lakes, oceans, and other bodies of water, plus underground water sources and water vapor in the air.

Almost 13 percent of the Earth's sea surface is covered by ice, most of it at the north and south poles. The amount of this ice and its distribution in the polar areas influence how much energy the Earth absorbs from the sun. This affects the Earth's climate.

The water in Earth's hydrosphere is always active. Water evaporates from the land, seas and other bodies of water, condensing in the Earth's atmosphere to form clouds. Then the water falls as rain or snow. That which falls on land is carried eventually to the sea and the cycle repeats itself. This cyclic action is called the Earth's hydrologic cycle.

EARTH'S STRUCTURE

Like the atmosphere, the Earth has several layers. The three primary layers are the crust, mantle, and core. The crust is a rigid, relatively thin layer. It can be as thin as 5 kilometers under the ocean, but as thick as 30 kilometers under large mountain ranges. The mantle is a dense, hot layer of semi-solid rock. This layer is approximately 2,900 kilometers thick. The mantle is hotter and denser than the crust because as you go from the outside, or crust of the earth, toward the inside, pressure and temperature within the Earth increase with depth. In the very center of the Earth is the core, which is almost twice as dense as the mantle and made primarily of metal, whereas the mantle and the crust are both composed of rockier substances. The core is made of two distinct parts: a 2,200 kilometers thick liquid outer core and a 1,250 kilometers thick solid inner core. As the Earth rotates on its axis, the liquid outer core also spins, creating the Earth's magnetic field.

SURFACE FEATURES AND GEOLOGICAL PROCESSES

The surface of the Earth is strongly impacted by the planet's internal structure. The upper part of the Earth's mantle is cooler and more rigid than the area of the mantle closest to the core and often behaves like an overlying crust. Together, the crust and this part of the mantle form a rigid layer of rock called the lithosphere. This layer is thinnest under the ocean and in volcanically active areas, like mountainous areas and those areas where two or more of the earth's tectonic plates meet. **Tectonic plates are plates formed out of the Earth's lithosphere.** These plates are moving and contain all the world's continents and oceans and rest on something called the asthenosphere. This zone is composed of hot, semi-solid material that softens and flows when subject to high temperature and pressure over time. The lithosphere is thought to float on the slowly flowing asthenosphere.

When the tectonic plates move on the asthenosphere, they often run into one another producing a variety of results including earthquakes and the rise of new mountains.

Other geological changes which strongly impact the Earth include volcanoes and erosion. When a volcano erupts and molten lava pours down from its crater, it is basically laying new rock. Entire islands are made from volcanic activity. The Hawaiian Islands are some of the best examples of volcanoes at work. The Big Island of Hawaii is constantly growing because of its largest volcano, Mauna Kea. When the lava flows from the volcano and into the sea, it lays new rock, extending the size of the island.

Erosion is when a rock or land is worn away by various processes such as the encroachment of glaciers and water or constantly blowing or strong wind. A good example of erosion is the Rocky Mountains. Though they look tall now, they were once twice the size they currently are. After millennia of water and wind, the Rockies have grown shorter and shorter.

Sometimes it is necessary to determine the slope of the land. To determine the slope, draw a line perpendicular to the lines of the slope. Measure your line according to the legend to see how many feet your line is. Divide the elevation change in feet by the length of your line in feet. Multiply your answer by 100 to figure out the percentage value for the hill.

GEOLOGICAL HISTORY OF THE EARTH

The Earth has a rich and complex geological history. The known history of Earth's geology is subdivided into three large chunks of time: Paleozoic, Mesozoic, and Cenozoic. These three categories are further divided into many categories that are separated by the species that evolved during them. The Paleozoic era spans from 550 to 355 million years ago. During that time, life on Earth evolved and began to diversify into prokaryotic and eukaryotic cells then further diversified into reptiles, amphibians, insects, fish, and other early species. Mammals did not evolve until very late in this era.

The Mesozoic era began 195 million years ago and lasted until about 60 million years ago. This era is commonly known as the age of reptiles due to the massive boom in the evolution in reptiles during that time. Dinosaurs also came into existence during the Mesozoic era.

The Cenozoic era, the age of mammals, began 60 million years ago and includes the geological present.

Prior to the time the dinosaurs evolved, all the landmass of the Earth was compressed into a single continent called Pangea. This continent, referred to as a "supercontinent," was surrounded by a gigantic ocean called Panthalassa.

About 180 million years ago, this continent began to break up. What caused this break up was the same thing that causes mountains to rise today: plate tectonics. The plates of the Earth, on their liquid asthenosphere, drifted away from each other, resulting in continental drift. In fact, the continents are still moving today.

When Pangea broke up, it gradually formed two new continents: Laurasia and Gondwanaland. Laurasia was comprised of the landmasses that are today North America, Greenland, Europe, and Asia. Gondwanaland was made up of what would later become Antarctica, Australia, India, and South America. It was not until North America split from the Eurasian Plate that the ocean Panthalassa began to break up.

Some people question how scientists know that the Earth was once one continent. The "Triple Junction" provides us with evidence. The Triple Junction was formed between the continents of Africa and South America. It was formed because of a three way split in the crust between the continents which allowed for massive lava flows. This split was the result of an upwelling of magma that broke the crust in three different directions and poured out lava across hundreds of square miles across both Africa and South America.

Rocks that were at the triple junction, which are now located at the West Central portion of Africa and the East Central portion of South America, are identical in mineral makeup and age. They were produced at the same time and same place. Therefore, the two continents must have been connected at one time.

ECOSYSTEMS

There are three parts to the layer around the Earth called the biosphere. The air is the atmosphere, the water is the hydrosphere and the minerals are the lithosphere. An ecosystem is a group of specific species of plants, animals and microbes that interact with each other and their environment, which includes temperature, seasons, moisture, etc.

Biomes and Terrestrial Communities

There are many different types of biomes. A biome is a major, classified, recognized community having well recognized plant and animal life. Here is a list of the most common ones:

- Desert – Few plants and animals make their home here. There is little or no rainfall; less than 10 inches a year makes an area a desert.
- Deep Sea – The deep sea ecosystems are unlike any others, the main reason being that it has developed in an area void of sunlight. Most ecosystems are dependent on the sun to survive. Organisms on the ocean floor take their energy directly from the earth through hydrothermal vents. Hydrothermal vents are essentially geysers found on the ocean floor. They send out geothermally heated water which the organisms thrive on.
- Coniferous Forest – This evergreen forest begins where tundra gives way to trees. This area is very cold in the winter time and pleasant during the summer.
- Grasslands – These areas are home to grazing animals. Grasslands grow where there is not enough moisture for trees.
- Deciduous Forest – This forest "turns" with the seasons; trees lose their leaves and there is snow. This biome experiences a full four seasons.
- Steppe – This is a large, flat area of land. Steppes are generally covered with short grasses less than one foot tall and receive 10 to 20 inches of rain a year. To put that in perspective, steppes receive more rain than deserts, but less than prairies. Steppes are mostly used to grow wheat or graze livestock.
- Tropical Rain Forest – These are found near the equator, are very hot and humid with a variety of different plants, animals and insects living together.
- Temperate Rain Forest – This a more temperate rain forest, and is slightly cooler than the tropical rain forest with less diversity of plant life, although it is still humid.
- Tundra – Tundra is found in the icy zones in the arctic. They have a very short growing period and no trees. Winter temperatures can be as cold as -70 Fahrenheit. It includes a thick layer of permafrost, a permanently frozen sub layer of soil.

- Aquatic – Water takes up more than 75% of the world's surface. There are many different types of aquatic biomes including salt water, fresh water and estuaries which are where the freshwater rivers or streams mix with the ocean.
- Savannah – Tropical grassland found in Africa, which includes a small amount of trees and large game.
- Taiga – This is the largest land biome. Cold in the winter and warm in the summer, it includes a large part of Canada and is home to moose and grizzly bear.
- Veldt – A veldt is similar to a steppe, but is used to describe the large, open grasslands in southern Africa.

The single greatest factor in determining what area a biome falls into is based on how much rainfall it experiences in a year.

GLOBAL CLIMATE AND THE GREENHOUSE EFFECT

AN INTRODUCTION

According to the National Academy of Sciences, the Earth's surface temperature has risen by about 1 degree Fahrenheit in the past century, with accelerated warming during the past two decades. There is new and stronger evidence that most of the warming over the last 50 years is attributable to human activities. Human activities have altered the chemical composition of the atmosphere through the buildup of greenhouse gases–primarily carbon dioxide, methane, and nitrous oxide. The heat trapping property of these gases is undisputed although uncertainties exist about exactly how Earth's climate responds to them.

OUR CHANGING ATMOSPHERE

Energy from the sun drives the Earth's weather and climate, and heats the Earth's surface; in turn, the Earth radiates energy back into space. Atmospheric greenhouse gases (water vapor, carbon dioxide, and other gases) trap some of the outgoing energy, retaining heat somewhat like the glass panels of a greenhouse.

Without this natural "greenhouse effect", temperatures would be much lower than they are now, and life as known today would not be possible. Instead, thanks to greenhouse gases, the Earth's average temperature is a more hospitable 60°F. However, problems may arise when the atmospheric concentration of greenhouse gases increases.

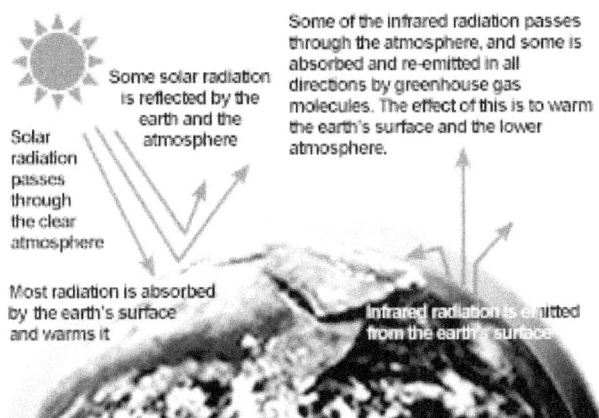

Since the beginning of the industrial revolution, atmospheric concentrations of carbon dioxide have increased nearly 30%, methane concentrations have more than doubled, and nitrous oxide concentrations have risen by about 15%. These increases have enhanced the heat trapping capability of the Earth's atmosphere. Sulfate aerosols, a common air pollutant, cool the atmosphere by reflecting light back into space; however, sulfates are short lived in the atmosphere and vary regionally.

Why are greenhouse gas concentrations increasing? Scientists generally believe that the combustion of fossil fuels and other human activities are the primary reason for the increased concentration of carbon dioxide. Plant respiration and the decomposition of organic matter release more than 10 times the CO2 released by human activities; but these releases have generally been in balance during the centuries leading up to the industrial revolution with carbon dioxide absorbed by terrestrial vegetation and the oceans.

What has changed in the last few hundred years is the additional release of carbon dioxide by human activities. Fossil fuels burned to run cars and trucks, heat homes and businesses, and power factories are responsible for about 98% of U.S. carbon dioxide emissions, 24% of methane emissions, and 18% of nitrous oxide emissions. Increased agriculture, deforestation, landfills, industrial production, and mining also contribute a significant share of emissions. In 1997, the United States emitted about one-fifth of total global greenhouse gases.

Estimating future emissions is difficult, because that calculation depends on demographic, economic, technological, policy, and institutional developments. Several emissions scenarios have been developed based on differing projections of these underlying factors. For example, by 2100, in the absence of emissions control policies, carbon dioxide concentrations are projected to be 30-150% higher than today's levels.

CHANGING CLIMATE

Global mean surface temperatures have increased 0.5-1.0°F since the late 19th century. The 20th century's 10 warmest years all occurred in the last 15 years of the century. Of these, 1998 was the warmest year on record. The snow cover in the Northern Hemisphere and floating ice in the Arctic Ocean have decreased. Globally, sea level has risen 4-8 inches over the past century. Worldwide precipitation over land has increased by about one percent. The frequency of extreme rainfall events has increased throughout much of the United States.

Increasing concentrations of greenhouse gases are likely to accelerate the rate of climate change. Scientists expect that the average global surface temperature could rise 1-4.5°F (0.6-2.5°C) in the next fifty years, and 2.2-10°F (1.4-5.8°C) in the next century, with significant regional variation. Evaporation will increase as the climate warms, which will increase average global precipitation. Soil moisture is likely to decline in many regions, and intense rainstorms are likely to become more frequent. Sea level is likely to rise two feet along most of the U.S. coast.

Calculations of climate change for specific areas are much less reliable than global calculations, and it is unclear whether regional climate will become more variable.

Scientists have identified that our health, agriculture, water resources, forests, wildlife and coastal areas are vulnerable to the changes that global warming may bring. But projecting what the exact impact will be over the 21st century remains very difficult. This is especially true when one asks how a local region will be affected.

Scientists are more confident about their projections for large scale areas (e.g., global temperature and precipitation change, average sea level rise) and less confident about projections for small scale areas (e.g., local temperature and precipitation changes, altered weather patterns, soil moisture changes). This is largely because the computer models used to forecast global climate change are still ill-equipped to simulate how things may change on smaller scales.

Some of the largest uncertainties are associated with events that pose the greatest risk to human societies. The IPCC cautions, "Complex systems, such as the climate system, can respond in non-linear ways and produce surprises." There is the possibility that a warmer world could lead to more frequent and intense storms, including hurricanes. Preliminary evidence suggests that, once hurricanes do form, they will be stronger if the oceans are warmer due to global warming. However, the jury is still out whether or not hurricanes and other storms will become more frequent.

More and more attention is being aimed at the possible link between El Niño events, the periodic warming of the equatorial Pacific Ocean, and global warming. Scientists are concerned that the accumulation of greenhouse gases could inject enough heat into Pacific waters such that El Niño events become more frequent and fierce. Here as well, research has not advanced far enough to provide conclusive statements about how global warming will affect El Niño scenarios.

LIVING WITH UNCERTAINTY

Like many pioneer fields of research, the current state of global warming science can't always provide definitive answers to our questions. There is certainty that human activities are rapidly adding greenhouse gases to the atmosphere, and that these gases tend to warm our planet. This is the basis for concern about global warming.

The fundamental scientific uncertainties are these: How much more warming will occur? How fast will this warming occur? And what are the potential adverse and beneficial effects? These uncertainties will be with us for some time, perhaps decades.

Global warming poses real risks. The exact nature of these risks remains uncertain. Ultimately, this is why we must use our best judgment, guided by the current state of science, to determine what the most appropriate response to global warming should be.

WHAT ARE GREENHOUSE GASES?

Some greenhouse gases occur naturally in the atmosphere, while others result from human activities. Naturally occurring greenhouse gases include water vapor, carbon dioxide, methane, nitrous oxide, and ozone. Certain human activities, however, add to the levels of most of these naturally occurring gases:

Carbon dioxide is released to the atmosphere when solid waste, fossil fuels (oil, natural gas, and coal), and wood and wood products are burned.

Methane is emitted during the production and transport of coal, natural gas, and oil. Methane emissions also result from the decomposition of organic wastes in municipal solid waste landfills, and the raising of livestock.

Nitrous oxide is emitted during agricultural and industrial activities, as well as during combustion of solid waste and fossil fuels.

Very powerful greenhouse gases that are not naturally occurring include hydrofluorocarbons (HFCs), perfluorocarbons (PFCs), and sulfur hexafluoride (SF6), which are generated in a variety of industrial processes.

Each greenhouse gas differs in its ability to absorb heat in the atmosphere. HFCs and PFCs are the most heat absorbent. Methane traps over 21 times more heat per molecule than carbon dioxide, and nitrous oxide absorbs 270 times more heat per molecule than carbon dioxide. Often, estimates of greenhouse gas emissions are presented in units of millions of metric tons of carbon equivalents (MMTCE), which weighs each gas by its GWP value, or Global Warming Potential.

WHAT ARE EMISSIONS INVENTORIES?

An emission inventory is an accounting of the amount of air pollutants discharged into the atmosphere. It is generally characterized by the following factors:

- the chemical or physical identity of the pollutants included,
- the geographic area covered,
- the institutional entities covered,
- the time period over which emissions are estimated, and
- the types of activities that cause emissions.

Emissions inventories are developed for a variety of purposes. Inventories of natural and anthropogenic emissions are used by scientists as inputs to air quality models, by policy makers to develop strategies and policies or track progress of standards, and by facilities and regulatory agencies to establish compliance records with allowable emission rates. A well-constructed inventory should include enough documentation and other data to allow readers to understand the underlying assumptions and to reconstruct the calculations for each of the estimates included.

WHAT ARE SINKS?

A sink is a reservoir that uptakes a chemical element or compound from another part of its cycle. For example, soil and trees tend to act as natural sinks for carbon – each year hundreds of billions of tons of carbon in the form of CO_2 are absorbed by oceans, soils, and trees.

POLLUTION

Pollution is the human caused addition of any material or energy which results in unwanted alterations. There are three main impacts to pollution:

- physical
- chemical
- biological

ENVIRONMENTAL RISK ASSESSMENT

Risk analysis began at the EPA or Environmental Protection Agency. Originally formed to research cancer risks associated with chemicals, this agency now does much more. They are responsible for risk analysis that includes:

- hazard assessment – linking hazards to its effects.
- dose-response assessment – how much (chemical/pollution) for how long?
- exposure assessment – which human groups are already exposed to the chemical, the dose, the length of time, and how they got exposed.
- risk characterization – how many will die?

ACID RAIN

"Acid rain" is a broad term used to describe several ways that acids fall out of the atmosphere. A more precise term is acid deposition, which has two parts: wet and dry.

Wet deposition refers to acidic rain, fog, and snow. As this acidic water flows over and through the ground, it affects a variety of plants and animals. The strength of the effects depends on many factors, including how acidic the water is, the chemistry and buffering capacity of the soils involved, and the types of fish, trees, and other living things that rely on the water.

Dry deposition refers to acidic gases and particles. About half of the acidity in the atmosphere falls back to earth through dry deposition. The wind blows these acidic particles and gases onto buildings, cars, homes, and trees. Dry deposited gases and particles can also be washed from trees and other surfaces by rainstorms. When that happens, the runoff water adds those acids to the acid rain, making the combination more acidic than the falling rain alone.

Prevailing winds blow the compounds that cause both wet and dry acid deposition across state and national borders, and sometimes over hundreds of miles.

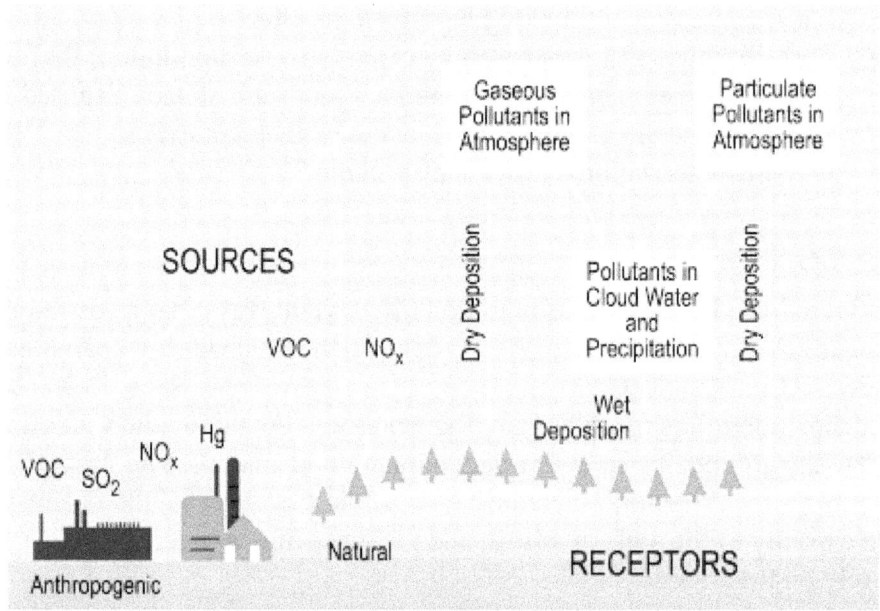

Scientists discovered, and have confirmed, that sulfur dioxide (SO2) and nitrogen oxides (NOx) are the primary causes of acid rain. In the US, about 2/3 of all SO2 and 1/4 of all NOx come from electric power generation that relies on burning fossil fuels like coal.

Acid rain occurs when these gases react in the atmosphere with water, oxygen, and other chemicals to form various acidic compounds. Sunlight increases the rate of most of these reactions. The result is a mild solution of sulfuric acid and nitric acid.

HOW DO WE MEASURE ACID RAIN?

Acid rain is measured using a scale called "pH." The lower a substance's pH, the more acidic it is. Pure water has a pH of 7.0. Normal rain is slightly acidic because carbon dioxide dissolves into it, so it has a pH of about 5.5. As of the year 2000, the most acidic rain falling in the US has a pH of about 4.3.

Acid rain's pH, and the chemicals that cause acid rain, are monitored by two networks, both supported by the EPA. Acidity in rain is measured by collecting samples of rain and measuring its pH. To find the distribution of rain acidity, weather conditions are monitored and rain samples are collected at sites all over the country. The areas of greatest acidity (lowest pH values) are located in the Northeastern United States. This pattern of high acidity is caused by the large number of cities, the dense population, and the concentration of power and industrial plants in the Northeast. In addition, the prevailing wind direction brings storms and pollution to the Northeast from the Midwest, and dust from the soil and rocks in the Northeastern United States is less likely to neutralize acidity in the rain.

WHAT ARE ACID RAIN'S EFFECTS?

Acid deposition has a variety of effects, including damage to forests and soils, fish and other living things, materials, and human health. Acid rain also reduces how far and how clearly we can see through the air, an effect called visibility reduction. Acid rain causes acidification of lakes and streams and contributes to the damage of trees at high elevations (for example, red spruce trees above 2,000 feet) and many sensitive forest soils. In addition, acid rain accelerates the decay of building materials and paints, including irreplaceable buildings, statues, and sculptures that are part of our nation's cultural heritage. Prior to falling to the earth, SO2 and NOx gases and their particulate matter derivatives, sulfates and nitrates, contribute to visibility degradation and harm public health.

7. BONUS SECTION

PHOTOSYNTHESIS

Photosynthesis is how plants take the energy from the sun and turn it into food for the plant. Energy starts with the sun that the plants absorb through the leaves. The chlorophyll in the leaf absorbs the sunlight and changes the water and carbon dioxide into oxygen and glucose. When the plants create sugars and starches, this combines atoms into a large atom. On the bottom of the leaves are the stomata, which are small openings. **The stomata are where transpiration takes place.** The stomata opens up to let air in and release oxygen. It also lets water out. Transpiration is the evaporation of water from plants when the stomata are open during photosynthesis. Photosynthesis is the process of a plant taking in Carbon Dioxide via the Stomata and creating food for the plant, and oxygen for the planet. Plants need water (H_2O) and carbon dioxide (CO_2) to make food via photosynthesis.

FOOD CHAIN

Plants are called **primary producers**. **Herbivores** are animals that eat plants. They are called **primary consumers** because they are what eat the plant. **Carnivores** are meat eaters and are **secondary consumers** because they eat a primary consumer. A **tertiary** consumer, is a carnivore that eats another carnivore. The chemical process from eating food results in free energy. Eating the plant breaks the energy bond.

PRENATAL GENETICS VOCABULARY

Amniocentesis is a test of the amniotic fluid to show any genetic problems in the baby.

Genetic engineering is adding desirable traits by inserting genes.

Artificial insemination is when the sperm is taken from a male and injected into the woman for conception.

Artificial implant is when a zygote (fertilized egg) is inserted into a uterus of someone unrelated. This is what is done with surrogate mothers. The mother hosts the baby which has the genes of a different mother and father.

Invitro fertilization is something that is done in the lab where the sperm and egg are combined and then implanted.

The **ovary** is the place where eggs are developed.

Ovulation is when the egg matures and breaks through the ovary. The sperm and egg meet in the fallopian tube. When the zygote (egg) does not attach to the sides, the lining is expelled. This is a woman's menstruation or period. Birth control pills signal to the body that an egg has not attached (even if it has) and the lining along with the egg are expelled.

Yolk sac is filled with food for the embryo.

Amniotic cavity is where the baby develops. The amniotic cavity can be found in ancordata/land vertebrae animals.

Placenta is the excretion track for the embryo. The mother is eating for two and excreting for two. Placentas are only found in mammals.

Allantois is holding excretion, choosing not to go.

Oxytocin is the chemical which causes the body to have contractions during pregnancy.

BODY ESSENTIALS

90% of the body is **water**.

Carbohydrates are sugars and starches.

Proteins are sources of essential amino acids.

Fats in general are storage for food. Your diet should be 20-30% from fat. Most people in the United States are at 40% or higher. The body combines glisorols with organic acids to make fat.

Vitamins are needed in small amounts. If you don't get enough, you can get scurvy. Scurvy is a lack of vitamin C. Another example of the body needing vitamins and minerals is when the body does not get enough calcium or potassium and there is an increase in muscle cramps and spasms. Minerals are used to build up specific tissues.

BACTERIA

Fermentation is when yeast is used to make alcohol. The yeast is actually alive and is considered an animal. Lactate fermenters are used with yogurt and cheese without oxygen.

Louis Pasteur was the father of microbiology. Since bacteria was discovered we have developed antibiotics and improved public sanitation.

DISEASE

Malaria is a serious, sometimes fatal disease caused by a parasite. Malaria is spread by mosquitoes who inject the parasite into the person's blood. In the past, DDT was used to exterminate mosquitoes until that was considered harmful to the human population.

A **virus** is a protein that mimics RNA and DNA. Viruses act as parasites, fooling the body into thinking they belong there. Some examples include the common cold, flu and measles, AIDS and Herpes.

Trichinosis is when parasites lay their eggs in the muscles of animals, mostly pork or chicken. A person can be infected by eating the bad meat.

Cancer happens when genetic material in a cell is damaged. The cell reproduces out of control and makes tumors that can then spread to other parts of the body. All tumors are bad. There are malignant tumors and benign tumors. Benign tumors are cells restricted to a specific area, and they are still bad as they show the body is not functioning normally.

Hypertension is when you have high blood pressure. This means that it is more difficult for the heart to pump blood.

Atherosclerosis is when plaque builds up and causes blockage.

Leukemia is a form of cancer, where you have too many white blood cells.

Menopause is not a disease, but it is something that afflicts most women as their body has chemical changes from their childbearing years. Women suffer from stress, hot flashes, perspiration and night sweats as their body adjusts and compensates to the new hormone levels. Some women participate in HRT, also known as hormone replacement therapy.

Hepatitis C is a disease with which 80% of people who have it experience no symptoms. Those that do experience symptoms may suffer jaundice, fatigue, dark urine, abdominal pain, and nausea. Those affected with Hepatitis C often need liver transplants.

Inherited sickness is any type of malady, sickness or disease that is inherited from the mother and father. These can include things like MS, AIDS and myopia. You can also inherit a tendency to get a certain disease based on your parental biological makeup.

Sickle Cell Anemia is a serious blood disease where the blood cells are shaped like the letter "c" instead of round like a donut. Sickle cells have an abnormal type of hemoglobin that makes the cells the odd shape. These cells can't travel through the body as well as other cells and can cause serious blockages of the vessels.

Osteoporosis is when the body hasn't stored enough calcium. The body takes the calcium from the bones, making them like Swiss cheese. These holes make the bones less stable, more brittle and easily breakable. Women and the elderly are more likely to be victims of this disease.

Emphysema results in the loss of elasticity of the lung tissue through long term exposure to chemicals, mainly tobacco smoke. The small balloon like alveoli in the lungs are damaged, collapse and the veins supporting them collapse as well. This results in the sufferer having a difficult time receiving adequate oxygen.

FUNCTIONS OF THE BODY

Exhale is the part of breathing when carbon dioxide is expelled from the body.

The thyroid regulates metabolism and needs iodine to function. Iodine was added to table salt for this purpose.

Adrenal glands give adrenaline to the body to support the "fight or flight" response.

Leukocytes are white blood cells and fight infection. **Erythrocytes** are red blood cells that bring oxygen to the different parts of the body.

There are different types of muscle tissue. They are:

- Epithelial
- Connective – Examples of this tissue are bone, cartilage and bone marrow
- Nervous

- Muscle – There are three types of muscle tissue:
  - Smooth: veins and arteries, areas around organs
  - Skeletal: striated, around skeleton, they help you move
  - Cardiac: in the heart, pump blood

Hepatic Portal Circulation regulates sugar level and amino acids, and includes the work of the intestines, spleen, pancreas and gall bladder.

When food is consumed by a person, here's what happens to it:
1. Stomach lining absorbs the food
2. Intestines pull out what your body wants from the food
3. Pancreas (which produces insulin and glucagon) gets the food ready to enter the blood stream
4. Liver (cleans the blood) produces bile that helps break down fatty foods
5. Gall Bladder saves up the bile from the liver
6. By the time it gets to the small intestine, all the chemical work has been done, so now the nutrient molecules can be absorbed.
7. Large intestine gets rid of solid waste

Exhaling is an excretion process. It gets rid of Hydrogen, Carbon and Oxygen. We get Hydrogen, Carbon and Oxygen from sugars. We get Nitrogen from proteins. Nitrogen is excreted. Fish and other aquatic creatures excrete Ammonia. They don't use kidneys but excrete through their scales.

Urea is waste from birds and reptiles. It looks like a white paste. Urea is the way they get rid of all their waste to conserve water. They do not create urine like mammals or amphibians. Human waste comes from the breakdown of amino acids in our food that we consume. Mammals and amphibians use their kidneys to create urine.

Birds, lizards, snakes and insects don't get a lot of water. They create Uric acid. There is no water in it. A paste is their feces/urine. All creatures that do this lay eggs.

TEMPERATURE REGULATION IN ANIMALS

Ecotherms: Animals whose body temperature is regulated by environment. For example, cold blooded animals and insects.

Endotherms: Animals who regulate their body temperature. Birds and mammals do this. Normal body functions need a certain temperature in which to operate.

ENDOCRINE SYSTEM

The endocrine system is a collection of glands that produce and store hormones. The hormones regulate metabolism, growth and sexual development. These glands release the hormones directly into the bloodstream to be sent to the rest of the organs in the body.

When there is an **organ transplant**, the white blood cells may attack the new organ because they see the organ as an invader.

Cornea transplant is the most successful transplant. Cornea is a protective covering for the eye and has no blood flow.

Echolocation: bats, whales and dolphins use this high-pitched sound, also known as ultrasound to navigate.

INSECTS

Pheromones or scents are used by insects to communicate with each other. They use these trail followings to follow each other and give warnings or give other messages. This can also be used to stake out territory and to signal sexual arousal.

Bees use a dance language where they dance in a figure eight pattern. They also wiggle their bottom to make other signals. They are social insects that live in colonies or hives and have different jobs like that of a worker bee or a queen bee.

Spiders and grasshoppers live by themselves, they are not social insects.

PLANTS

Plant cells have a cell wall. Animal cells do not.

Vascular cambium goes all the way up and to the veins of the leaves. It sends out all minerals and water to all parts of the tree. Transpiration is the evaporation of water from plants from when the stomata in the cell is open during photosynthesis. Xylem is tree sap.

Stoma is the opening in leaves where transpiration takes place. Water evaporates from the stoma sucking up the xylem into the leaves. During the fall the vascular cambium dries up and dies. In the spring a new vascular cambium grows, that is why trees get fatter. Trees grow from the top up.

Waxy coating on plants and stoma openings help in hot climates to keep water in. Animals and bees pollinate the flowers and plants by carrying the pollen on their bodies as they go from plant to plant.

FLOWER REPRODUCTIVE PARTS

A- Stigma, sticky and traps pollen grains
B- Style, tube leading to the ovary
C- Ovary
D- Petal
E- Sepal, the outer flower structure.
F- Receptacle
G- Stalk, supports the supporting the flower.
H- Filament, supports the anther
I- Anther, produces pollen grains that contain sperm cells.

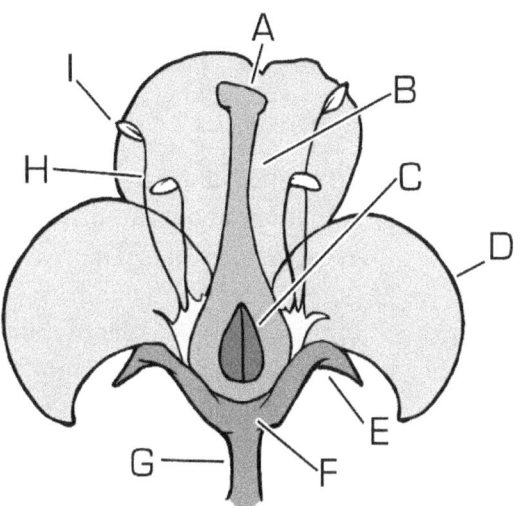

Stamen - the male organ
- Anther
- Filament

Pistil - the female organ
- Stigma
- Style
- Ovary
- Ovules

SCIENTIFIC METHOD

Scientific Method is four steps:

1. Gather information
2. Generate hypothesis
3. Test hypothesis
4. Revise

If a study goes wrong or has an error in it, you can draw no conclusion.

ANIMAL BREEDING

Pure bred dogs are dogs that are only bred with their same type of dog for a favorable trait or look. This can cause health problems for the dogs as sometimes the owners are inbreeding the animals. This results in Saint Bernards having poor hip bones. There are laws against human inbreeding for that same reason, because it can cause major health problems and deformations.

Polygenetic: two pairs of genes are used to determine what is passed on.

RH FACTOR

Rh factor is something everyone has. You are either Rh negative or positive. If the baby has Rh positive blood and the mother is Rh negative it could cause the mother's cells to attack the baby. To fix this, injections are given in the doctor's office or hospital.

ALBINISM

From the National Organization of Albinism and Hyperpigmentation, here is some information about the disease: "People with albinism have little or no pigment in their eyes, skin, or hair. They have inherited genes that do not make the usual amounts of a pigment called melanin. When both parents carry the gene, and neither parent has albinism, there is a one in four chance at each pregnancy that the baby will be born with albinism. This type of inheritance is called autosomal recessive inheritance."[1] People who have it are sometimes called Albinos. Albinism can affect people from all races.

CHARLES DARWIN

Charles Darwin sailed a ship around the world called the HMS Beagle. He found fossils of extinct organisms. He also went to the Galapagos Islands. Darwin also studied finches. He discovered that they had different beak sizes. It was noticing that that helped Darwin realize natural selection. Bigger beaks helped the finches to survive and so he learned of evolution and natural selection. Natural selection is when nature determines that a species will or will not survive. For example, an animal that is not fast enough to run from a predator will not survive to procreate, so eventually (over hundreds or thousands of years) the animals left to procreate are the fastest and have inherited that ability from their parents.

Physics

1. THE BASICS OF MOTION

Dynamics is the study of the relationship between motion and the forces affecting motion. **Force** causes motion to start or to stop, to change direction, or to change speed. The **mass** of a body at rest is the same at all points in the universe because mass is the quantity of matter in the body. Earth's gravity pulls objects towards the Earth. Therefore, the **weight** of an object is its mass times the acceleration due to the gravity acting upon it (**W = mg**). The units for mass are derivatives of grams (kilograms, micrograms, etc.) and the unit for weight is the Newton.

The more mass an object has, the greater the pull of gravity upon it. As the object increases its distance from the surface of the Earth, the pull of gravity on it lessens. For example, a rocket triples its distance from Earth so the gravitational pull on the rocket becomes 1/9 as much.

Throwing a ball puts it into motion. How fast it travels is its **speed** which is measured as the **distance** it travels divided by the **time** it took to travel that far, or s = d/t, which is usually kilometers per hour or meters per second. Velocity refers to both the speed and the direction of movement. A speed can be calculated for a specific distance or a specific amount of time or it can be an average speed for a total distance in a total amount of time.

> Example: *A runner completes 5 kilometers of a 10K race in 20 minutes and the second half of the race in 25 minutes. What is his speed for the first half? What is his speed for the second half? What is his average speed?*
>
> His first half speed: s = 5 km/20 min = 0.25 km/min
> His second half speed: s = 5 km/25 min = 0.20 km/min
> His average speed: s = 10 km/45 min = 0.22 km/min

If you are going to drive a car, you start from being parked. The car at rest is at a speed of zero. You apply pressure to the accelerator or gas pedal and the car starts moving. In less than a minute, it may reach a speed of 50 km per hour. The equation for **acceleration** is:

$$a = v_2 - v_1 / t \text{ where } v_1 \text{ is the beginning velocity of } 0$$

Likewise, when you come to a red light, you apply the brake and use the force of braking to decelerate to zero. To calculate the **deceleration**, you would use the same equation as for acceleration, but v2 would be zero instead of v1 being zero. Acceleration and deceleration are rates at which speed changes.

Acceleration is defined as the rate of change of velocity with respect to time. It is always represented with both a magnitude and a direction. Magnitude refers to the size of the change. For example, 1, 5, or 6 are representative of different magnitudes. Direction is indicated using either a positive or negative sign. Although direction is not absolute (or always the same) it is typically standard to consider up or to the right to be positive, and down or to the left to be negative unless otherwise indicated. The units of acceleration are meters per second per second, m/s/s, or meters per second squared m/s^2. Either is equally acceptable, although m/s^2 is simpler to write and is more commonly used.

As mentioned previously, acceleration is used to describe a change in velocity; however, a positive acceleration does not always indicate that an object's speed is increasing. If acceleration and velocity are in the same direction (both are positive or both are negative) then the velocity is increasing. On the other hand, if acceleration and velocity are in opposite directions (one is positive and the other is negative) then the object will move slower with time. If an object moves with a constant velocity over time, it must have an acceleration of zero.

Because acceleration is defined as the rate of change of velocity with respect to time, it must be measured as time changes. Acceleration is determined as $\Delta v/\Delta t$ (Δ is the Greek letter delta and represents change). Therefore, if an object accelerates from 3 m/s to 9 m/s in 3 seconds, its acceleration was (9-3)/3 or 2 m/s2.

There are a number of equations which relate acceleration to other values, such as position, time and velocity. These can be useful in doing calculations. These equations are referred to as kinematics equations. It is extremely important to remember that these equations only apply in situations where acceleration is constant. This is referred to as uniform motion, and is often assumed to make situations easier to analyze. However, if acceleration changes with time then these equations cannot be used.

The three most basic kinematics equations are (1) $v = v_o + at$, (2) $\Delta x = (1/2)at^2 + v_o t$, (3) $v = 2a(\Delta x) + v_o^2$. In the equations, v_o represents initial velocity (if an object starts from rest, this value can be ignored), and Δx represents change in position, or distance.

One of the most common situations in which these equations are used is when an object is in freefall, which means that it is falling under the influence of gravity. It is a common situation to use because acceleration due to gravity is always a constant 9.8 m/s2 for objects of any size or mass. For an example of the kinematics equations in use, consider this problem: A block is dropped, from rest, from the top of a large building. Ignoring air friction, determine is its velocity after 3 seconds, and how far has it fallen. Because the question tells us that there is no air friction, we know that the only force is gravity, and that it must be falling with an acceleration of 9.8 m/s^2. Because it is falling from rest we know that initial velocity is 0. Using this information, and the fact that it tells us t=3, we can simply plug the values into the proper equations. Using the first equation we determine that $v = v_o + at = 0 + (9.8)(3) = 29.4$ m/s. Using the second equation we determine that $\Delta x = (1/2)at^2 + v_o t = (1/2)(9.8)(3^2)+(0)(3) = 44.1 + 0 = 44.1$ m.

2. VECTORS

Quantities which have only a numeral and a unit such as mass or volume are said to be scalar quantities. When a body moves from one location to another, it is called displacement. A displacement has both a magnitude (how much) with a numeral and a unit and a direction. Quantities with magnitude and direction are vector quantities and can be represented, added, and subtracted graphically. If there are two vectors in the same direction, add them together. If there are two vectors in opposite directions, subtract the smaller from the larger.

10 mm East	25 mm East	25 mm East
		10 mm West
10 mm + 25 mm = 35 mm E		25 mm – 10 mm = 15 mm East

Vectors are not always this simple. However, it always helps to make a scaled drawing. If possible place the vectors head to tail. If they cannot simply be added or subtracted, you may need to use geometrical calculations based on the properties of right triangles:

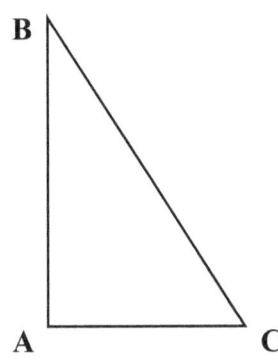

Angle A is the right angle. BC is the hypotenuse. To get the length of AB if you know angle B, use a cosine or to get the length of AB if you know angle C, use a sine. Sine or sin C = opposite side/hypotenuse = AB/BC

Cosine or cos B = adjacent side/hypotenuse = AB/BC

Tangent B or tan B = opposite side/adjacent side = AC/AB

*Displacement, velocity, and acceleration are vector quantities.

3. THE BASICS OF MOTION

NEWTON'S LAWS OF MOTION

The tendency of a moving object to keep moving is called inertia. When you stop your car suddenly, your body keeps going forward through inertia. If a body is not moving, it takes force to make it move. This, too, is inertia. Sir Isaac Newton (1642-1727) stated three laws which explain the way objects move.

Newton's first law of motion is also called the law of inertia. It states that an object at rest will remain at rest and an object in motion will remain in motion at a constant velocity unless acted upon by an external force. For example, a sailboat floats on a lake. The sails are put up. A breeze exerts a force on the sails. The boat moves. The skipper moves the rudder right or left to change direction. The force of the water on the rudder makes the boat turn.

Newton's second law of motion states that if a net force acts on an object, it will cause the object to accelerate. The relationship between force and motion is Force equals mass times acceleration. (F = ma). Acceleration of an object increases as the amount of force causing the acceleration increases. Heavier objects (such as a moving van) need more force than lighter objects (such as a sports car) in order to accelerate or decelerate.

Newton's third law states that for every action there is an equal and opposite reaction. Therefore, if an object exerts a force on another object, that second object exerts an equal and opposite force on the first. For instance, a boat may be forced by the currents to drift away but an equal and opposite force is exerted by a rope holding it to a dock.

Sample Test Questions

1) Asteroids are majorly located in the

    A) Asteroid belt between Mars and Jupiter
    B) Near the orbit of the Earth
    C) Asteroid belt near the Sun
    D) Near the moon
    E) Asteroid belt between Jupiter and Venus

The correct answer is: A:) Asteroid belt between Mars and Jupiter.

2) As opposed to the Earth, the moon has craters because of

    A) Displacement of its surface
    B) Chemical composition of the land
    C) Meteoric impacts on its surface
    D) Volcanic eruptions blasting holes
    E) Changing temperature

The correct answer is: C:) Meteoric impacts on its surface. Impact craters were formed a billion years ago when meteorites, asteroids and comets struck its surface. The Earth on the other hand has an atmosphere which causes asteroids to burn up before they touch the surface.

3) A correct example of a balanced chemical equation is

   A) $2Fe_2O_3 + 3C \rightarrow 4Fe + 3CO_4$
   B) $2Fe_2O_3 + 3C \rightarrow 2Fe + 3CO_3$
   C) $2Fe_2O_3 + 3C \rightarrow 2Fe + 3CO_2$
   D) $2Fe_2O_3 + 3C \rightarrow 4Fe + 3CO_3$
   E) $2Fe_2O_3 + 3C \rightarrow 4Fe + 3CO_2$

The correct answer is: E:) $2Fe_2O_3 + 3C \rightarrow 4Fe + 3CO_2$. The hydrogen (H) atoms are balanced because of the coefficient 2 in front of H2O, there a total of 4 oxygen (O) atoms on the product side.

4) The meaning of refraction is

   A) Moving of energy at an extremely rapid rate
   B) Change in speed of light
   C) Bending of a wave when it enters a medium with different wave
   D) Movement of waves made of oscillating magnetic and electric fields
   E) Reflection of light

The correct answer is: C:) Bending of a wave when it enters a medium with different wave. The refraction of light when it goes through from a fast medium to a slow medium bends the light ray toward the normal to the boundary between the two mediums.

5) Cellulose is a part of a cell wall which is essential in

   A) Pathway of energy
   B) Excretion
   C) Energy storage
   D) Protection and structure
   E) Power house of the cell

The correct answer is: D:) Protection and structure. The plant cell wall is made up of cellulose. Cellulose is considered a complex sugar because it is used in both protection and structure. Cellulose is also composed of structural carbohydrates.

6) Red blood cells are colored red because of

   A) Platelets
   B) Leukocytes
   C) Hemoglobin
   D) Plasma
   E) Erythropoietin

The correct answer is: C:) Hemoglobin. We have a protein called hemoglobin in our red blood cells. This protein contains four iron atoms that bind to oxygen. The iron component is what makes our blood colored red and how oxygen is carried around our blood stream.

7) Fraunhoffer lines in the solar spectrum correspond to radiation

   A) Emitted by the inner part of the sun but absorbed by its outer atmosphere
   B) Not absorbed due to imperfect instruments
   C) Not emitted by the sun
   D) Emitted by the sun but absorbed by the earth's atmosphere
   E) Emitted by stars

The correct answer is A:) Emitted by the inner part of the sun but absorbed by its outer atmosphere.

8) The birds Charles Darwin studied and influenced his research in natural selection were

   A) Condors
   B) Finches
   C) Puffins
   D) Dippers
   E) Cranes

The correct answer is B:) Finches.

9) Which of the following are NOT social insects?

   A) Bees
   B) Ants
   C) Spiders
   D) Termites
   E) Wasps

The correct answer is C:) Spiders.

10) What is produced, on heating a mixture of potassium cyanate and ammonium chloride?

   A) Urea
   B) Ethanamide
   C) Methanamide
   D) Ethanamine
   E) Potassium chloride

The correct answer is A:) Urea.

11) Which of the following is not part of the earth's internal structure?

   A) Lithosphere
   B) Crust
   C) Ionosphere
   D) Mantle
   E) Core

The correct answer is C:) Ionosphere.

12) Which of the following terms is used to define atoms of different elements, which contain the same number of neutrons?

   A) Isotones
   B) Isotopes
   C) Isobars
   D) Isomers
   E) None of these

The correct answer is A:) Isotones.

13) General electronic configuration for d-block elements is?

   A) (n-1)d1-5ns1-2
   B) (n-1)d1-10ns1-2
   C) (n-1)d1-10ns0-2
   D) (n-1)d1- 5ns0-1
   E) None of these

The correct answer is C:) (n-1)d1-10ns0-2.

14) Which of the following alkali metal halide has the lowest lattice energy?

   A) LiF
   B) KBr
   C) NaCl
   D) CsI
   E) Cacl

The correct answer is D:) CsI.

15) Metal ions like Ag+, Cu2+ etc. act as?

   A) Bronsted acids
   B) Lewis acids
   C) Bronsted base
   D) Lewis base
   E) None of these

The correct answer is B:) Lewis acids.

16) The oxidation number of oxygen in OF2 is?

   A) +2
   B) -2
   C) +1
   D) -1
   E) 1

The correct answer is A:) +2.

17) When a ¹ b¹ c, a ¹ b ¹ g ¹ 90°, define the type of unit cell?

   A) Tetragonal
   B) Rhombic
   C) Monoclinic
   D) Triclinic
   E) None of these

The correct answer is D:) Triclinic.

18) The three axes of a crystal lattice are mutually perpendicular but all lattice parameters are unequal. The crystal is

   A) Cubic
   B) Tetragonal
   C) Orthorhombic
   D) Hexagonal
   E) Pentagonal

The correct answer is C:) Orthorhombic.

19) Conductors, insulators and semi-conductors differ from each other due to property of

   A) Ability of the current they carry
   B) Formation of crystal lattice
   C) Binding energy of their electrons
   D) Mutual width of their energy gaps
   E) None of these

The correct answer is D:) Mutual width of their energy gaps.

20) Fermi energy level is

   A) The minimum energy of electrons at 0 K
   B) The maximum energy of electrons at 273 K
   C) The maximum energy of electrons at 0 K
   D) The minimum energy of electrons at 273 K
   E) The minimum energy of electrons at 275K

The correct answer is C:) The maximum energy of electrons at 0 K.

21) That which can be used for measuring a rapidly changing temperature is a

   A) Thermocouple thermometer
   B) Gas thermometer
   C) Platinum resistance thermometer
   D) Vapor pressure thermometer
   E) Both A and D

The correct answer is A:) Thermocouple thermometer.

22) Expansion during heating

    A) Occurs only in a solid
    B) Increases the weight of a material
    C) Decreases the density of the material
    D) Occurs at the same rate for all liquids and solids
    E) Occurs only in gases

The correct answer is C:) Decreases the density of the material.

23) A ring-shaped piece of metal is heated. If the material expands, the hole will

    A) Expand
    B) Contract
    C) Expand or contract depending on the width of the ring
    D) Expand or contract depending on the value of the coefficient of expansion
    E) Will have no effect

The correct answer is A:) Expand.

24) A solid ball of metal has a spherical cavity inside it. The ball is heated. The volume of cavity will

    A) Decrease
    B) Increase
    C) Remain unchanged
    D) Have its shape changed
    E) Its weight will decrease

The correct answer is B:) Increase.

25) If a bimetallic strip is heated it will

    A) Bend toward the metal with lower thermal expansion coefficient
    B) Bend toward the metal with higher thermal expansion coefficient
    C) Twist itself into a helix
    D) Have no bending
    E) It will expand linearly

The correct answer is A:) Bend toward the metal with lower thermal expansion coefficient.

26) On heating a liquid of coefficient of cubical expansion a in a container having coefficient of linear expansion a/3, the level of liquid in the container will

   A) Rise
   B) Fall
   C) Will remain almost stationary
   D) It is difficult to say
   E) Will rise at first and then remain constant at certain level

The correct answer is C:) Will remain almost stationary.

27) When water is heated from 0°C to 10°C, its volume

   A) Increases
   B) Does not change
   C) First decreases and then increases
   D) First increases and then decreases
   E) None of the above

The correct answer is C:) First decreases and then increases.

28) A beaker is filled with water at 4°C. At one time the temperature is increased by few degrees above 4°C and at another time it is decreased by few degrees below 4°C. One shall observe that

   A) The level remains constant in each case
   B) Water overflows in both cases
   C) Water overflows in the latter case, while comes down in the previous case
   D) In previous case water overflows while in latter case its levels comes down
   E) Nothing happens

The correct answer is B:) Water overflows in both cases.

29) A bimetal made of copper and iron strips welded together is straight at room temperature. It is held vertically in the hand so that the iron strip is towards the left hand and copper strip is towards the right hand side. This bimetal is then heated by flame. The bimetal strip will

   A) Remain straight
   B) Bend towards right
   C) Bend towards left
   D) Have no change
   E) Its thermal expansion coefficient will increase

The correct answer is C:) Bend towards left.

30) Which planet is the farthest from Earth?

   A) Jupiter
   B) Saturn
   C) Uranus
   D) Neptune
   E) Venus

The correct answer is D:) Neptune.

31) When a convergent beam of light is incident on a plane mirror, the image formed is

   A) Upright and real
   B) Upright and virtual
   C) Inverted and virtual
   D) Inverted and real
   E) Opaque

The correct answer is C:) Inverted and virtual.

32) A plane mirror reflecting a ray of incident light is rotated through an angle 6 about an axis through the point of incidence in the plane of the mirror perpendicular to the plane of incidence, then

   A) The reflected ray does not rotate
   B) The reflected ray rotates through an angle 0
   C) The reflected ray rotates through an angle 29
   D) The incident ray is fixed
   E) The reflected ray rotates through an angle 10

The correct answer is C:) The reflected ray rotates through an angle 29.

33) A monochromatic beam of light passes from a denser medium to a rarer medium. As a result

   A) Its velocity increases
   B) Its velocity decreases
   C) Its frequency decreases
   D) Its frequency increases
   E) Its wavelength decreases

The correct answer is A:) Its velocity increases.

34) When a ray of light enters a glass slab from air

   A) Its wavelength decreases
   B) Its wavelength increases
   C) Its frequency increases
   D) Its frequency decreases
   E) Neither wavelength nor frequency changes

The correct answer is A:) Its wavelength decreases.

35) While analyzing the spectrum of any specific galaxy, when they are moving away from each other, the speed of spectrum is what? Assume Ao = 5000A4 and X\ = 5050A4 are

   A) 30000 km sec"l
   B) 3000 km sec"l
   C) 300 km sec"l
   D) 30 km sec"l
   E) None of the above

The correct answer is B:) 3000 km sec"1.

36) Proxima Centauri, which is the nearest star, appears after how many years?

   A) 1.3 years ago
   B) 2.3 years ago
   C) 3.3 years ago
   D) 4.3 years ago
   E) 1 year ago

The correct answer is D:) 4.3 years ago.

37) Where are blood cells made?

   A) Liver
   B) Kidneys
   C) Heart
   D) Lungs
   E) Bone marrow

The correct answer is E:) Bone marrow.

38) X-ray telescopes have what shape?

   A) They have barrel-like shape
   B) They have dish-like shape
   C) They have circular shape
   D) They have elliptical shape
   E) They have disk-like shape

The correct answer is A:) They have barrel-like shape.

39) Neutron has a molar mass of

   A) 1.086650 g/mol
   B) 1.86650 g/mol
   C) 1.0086650 g/mol
   D) 1.00086650 g/mol
   E) 1.0065g/mol

The correct answer is C:) 1.0086650 g/mol.

40) The testing of carbon dioxide present in the air can be done by?

   A) By passing air through limewater
   B) By passing air through cold water
   C) By passing air through hot water
   D) By adding soda in cold water
   E) All of these

The correct answer is A:) By passing air through limewater.

41) The major portion of earth's surface is covered with?

   A) Trees
   B) Animals
   C) Waters
   D) Both (b) and(c)
   E) None of these

The correct answer is C:) Waters.

42) The temperature of the land is regulated by which two processes?

   A) Oceanic currents and conduction current
   B) Transversal currents and convection current
   C) Oceanic currents and convection current
   D) Convection current only
   E) None of these

The correct answer is C:) Oceanic currents and convection current.

43) The location of Mid Atlantic ridge is at?

   A) Bottom of Earth's surface
   B) Bottom of Atlantic Ocean
   C) Surface of Atlantic Ocean
   D) Mid of Atlantic Ocean
   E) None of the above

The correct answer is D:) Mid of Atlantic Ocean.

44) The dissolution of covalent compounds in water is by the formation of?

   A) Oxygen bond
   B) Carbon bond
   C) Nitrogen bond
   D) Hydrogen bond
   E) Both carbon and nitrogen

The correct answer is D:) Hydrogen bond.

45) The main composition compounds of acid rain are?

   A) Sulphuric acid and acetic acid
   B) Sulphuric acid and nitric acid
   C) Nitric acid and acetic acid
   D) Nitric and phosphate acid
   E) None of these

The correct answer is B:) Sulphuric acid and nitric acid.

46) The deformation of Earth's crust is carried out under which field of geology?

   A) Metatonic
   B) Pectonic
   C) Tectonic
   D) Hypotonic
   E) None of these

The correct answer is C:) Tectonic.

47) Transform fault occurs at

   A) San Andreas Fault of California
   B) Anatolian fault of northern Turkey
   C) At Pacific Bay
   D) Both of (A) and (B)
   E) None of these

The correct answer is C:) At Pacific Bay.

48) Name the three identifiable types of earthquake movements or shock waves

   A) P, Q, and R wave
   B) P, S, and L wave
   C) S, Q, and L wave
   D) P, R and L wave
   E) None of these

The correct answer is B:) P, S, and L wave.

49) With increase in population, the demand for fresh water has?

   A) Decreased
   B) Increased
   C) Remained constant
   D) Not known
   E) None of these

The correct answer is B:) Increased.

50) Which land alteration from human activities affects the hydrological cycle?

   A) Biological characteristics
   B) Physical characteristics
   C) Chemical characteristics
   D) All of these
   E) None of these

The correct answer is D:) All of these.

51) Land slope occurs in which way?

   A) Upward west to the east
   B) Upward east to the west
   C) Downward west to the east
   D) Downward east to the west
   E) Upward north to the south

The correct answer is C:) Downward west to the east.

52) Ozone is an an _____ of oxygen?

   A) Isotope
   B) Unitope
   C) Allotrope
   D) Element
   E) None of these

The correct answer is C:) Allotrope.

53) Which era is dubbed as the age of prokaryotic microbes?

   A) Phanerozoic
   B) Archean
   C) Proterozoic
   D) Prokaryotic era
   E) Precambrian

The correct answer is E:) Precambrian.

54) What part of the brain is responsible for speech?

   A) Hippocampus
   B) Corpus callosum
   C) Temporal lobe
   D) Parietal lobes
   E) Frontal lobe

The correct answer is E:) Frontal lobe.

55) Pithecanthropus erectus fossil was found in

   A) Texas
   B) Japan
   C) Java
   D) China
   E) India

The correct answer is C:) Java.

56) The correct sequence of stages in the evolution of the modern man (Homo sapiens) is

   A) Homo erectus, Australopithecus, Neanderthal man, Cro-Magnon man, modern man
   B) Neanderthal man, Australopithecus, Cro-Magnon man, Homo erectus, modern man
   C) Australopithecus, Homo erectus, Neanderthal man, Cro-Magnon man, modern man
   D) Australopithecus, Neanderthal man, Cro-Magnon man, Homo erectus, modern man
   E) Homo erectus, Neanderthal man, Australopithecus, Cro-Magnon man, modern man

The correct answer is C:) Australopithecus, Homo erectus, Neanderthal man, Cro-Magnon man, modern man.

57) Which of the following changes involved is irrelevant in the evolution of man?

   A) Increase in the ability to communicate with others and develop community behavior
   B) Perfection of hand for tool making
   C) Change of diet from hard nuts and hard roots to soft food
   D) Ability to speak
   E) Loss of tail

The correct answer is E:) Loss of tail.

58) Which fossil man has been known from the Shivalik hills in India?

   A) Zinjanthropus
   B) Ramapithecus
   C) Pithecanthropus
   D) Sinanthropus
   E) None of the above

The correct answer is B:) Ramapithecus.

59) What does HIV stand for?

   A) Human Insufficiency Virus
   B) Helper Insufficiency Virus
   C) Helper Immunodeficiency Virus
   D) Human Immunodeficiency Virus
   E) None of the above

The correct answer is D:) Human Immunodeficiency Virus.

60) Which of the following is the direct ancestor of Homo sapiens?

   A) Homo erectus
   B) Homo-sapiens Neanderthals
   C) Ramapithecus
   D) Australopithecus
   E) Pithecanthropus

The correct answer is A:) Homo erectus.

61) Which of the following statements is correct regarding the evolution of mankind?

   A) Australopithecus was living in Australia
   B) Neanderthal man and Cro-Magnon man were living at the same time
   C) Homo erectus is preceded by Homohabilis
   D) Both A and B
   E) None of these

The correct answer is B:) Neanderthal man and Cro-Magnon man were living at the same time.

62) Common origin of man and chimpanzee is best shown by

   A) Dental formula
   B) Cranial capacity
   C) Chromosome number in binding
   D) Binocular vision
   E) None of the above

The correct answer is B:) Cranial capacity.

63) The link between 'Homo erectus and Australopithecus' is

   A) Dryopithicus
   B) Ramapithecus
   C) Homo habilis
   D) Homo-sapiens
   E) Zinjanthropus

The correct answer is C:) Homo habilis.

64) Descent of man and selection in relation to man is the work of

   A) Darwin
   B) Lamarck
   C) Linnaeus
   D) Mendel
   E) Elvis

The correct answer is A:) Darwin.

65) On Fl heterozygous red flowered plants, the R, generation has both red and white flowered plants; it proves

   A) Blended inheritance
   B) Law of Independent assortment
   C) Law of segregation
   D) Law of dominance
   E) Pollination

The correct answer is C:) Law of segregation.

66) The science that deals with the study of resemblances and differences between the parents and their progeny is called

   A) Genetics
   B) Biology
   C) Heredity
   D) Variation
   E) Biochemistry

The correct answer is A:) Genetics.

67) The cross of F1 individuals with homozygous recessive parent is called

   A) Test cross
   B) Back cross
   C) Reciprocal cross
   D) Double cross
   E) None of these

The correct answer is A:) Test cross.

68) Sickle cell anemic persons die normally due to

   A) Lethal genes
   B) Inhibitory genes
   C) Pleiotropic genes
   D) Both A and C
   E) Both A and B

The correct answer is E:) Both A and B.

69) If drooping ear is dominant over straight ear, the percentage of drooping ear offspring would be (when both the parents have straight ear)

   A) 50%
   B) 100%
   C) 75%
   D) 0%
   E) 25%

The correct answer is D:) 0%.

70) In a cross Tt x Tt, the percentage of offspring produced having the same phenotype as the parents would be

   A) 50%
   B) 100%
   C) 25%
   D) 75%
   E) 0%

The correct answer is A:) 50%.

71) The condition in which the allelomorphic genes are expressed partially when present together in the hybrid is called

   A) Pleiotropy
   B) Incomplete dominance
   C) Quantitative inheritance
   D) Epistasis
   E) None of the above

The correct answer is B:) Incomplete dominance.

72) When a tall plant is crossed with a dwarf plant, the ratio of pure tall and pure dwarf in F2 generation will be:

   A) 2:1
   B) 3:1
   C) 9:3
   D) 4:1
   E) 1:1

The correct answer is E:) 1:1.

73) The gene that in homozygous condition results in the production of a non-viable progeny is called

   A) Lethal gene
   B) Epi static gene
   C) Complementary gene
   D) Inhibitory gene
   E) Pleiotropic genes

The correct answer is A:) Lethal gene.

74) The condition of having only one allele of a pair in a cross or individual is called

   A) Incomplete dominance
   B) Homozygous
   C) Complementary inheritance
   D) Complete inheritance
   E) Hemizygous

The correct answer is E:) Hemizygous.

75) The interphase nucleus has:

   A) A porous single membrane
   B) A porous double membrane
   C) A non-porous single membrane
   D) A non-porous double membrane
   E) No membrane

The correct answer is B:) A porous double membrane.

76) Photosynthetic units are:

   A) Oxysome
   B) Peroxysome
   C) Dictyosome
   D) Quantasome
   E) Neosome

The correct answer is D:) Quantasome.

77) Obiquinone is:

   A) Metabolic of Krebs cycle
   B) Electron carrier
   C) Anti-malarial drug
   D) Antibiotic
   E) Intermediary product of glycolysis

The correct answer is E:) Intermediary product of glycolysis.

78) Cancer cells live a parasitic life and drain off much energy from the host organism, because ATP available per lactate to glucose conversion is deficient by:

   A) 2 ATP molecules
   B) 4 ATP molecules
   C) 6 ATP molecules
   D) 30 ATP molecules
   E) 5 ATP molecules

The correct answer is D:) 30 ATP molecules.

79) The idea that cells comes from pre-existing cells was proposed by:

   A) Leeuwenhock
   B) Virchow
   C) Robert Hooke
   D) Louis Pasteur
   E) Thomas Crook

The correct answer is D:) Louis Pasteur.

80) Acid rain does NOT fall to the earth in what form?

   A) Fog
   B) Rain
   C) Snow
   D) Sleet
   E) None of the above

The correct answer is E:) None of the above. Acid rain can occur in fog, rain and snow.

81) Cell-plate in plant cell is formed of:

   A) Pectin
   B) Phragmosome
   C) Lecithin
   D) Suberin
   E) Pencilin

The correct answer is B:) Phragmosome.

82) Endomitosis results in:

   A) Haploidy
   B) Diploidy
   C) Aneuploidy
   D) Euploidy
   E) None of the above

The correct answer is C:) Aneuploidy.

83) What type of cells does Human Immunodeficiency Virus (HIV) attack?

   A) Helper T Cells
   B) Cytotoxic T Cells
   C) Memory B Cells
   D) Memory T Cells
   E) None of the above

The correct answer is A:) Helper T Cells. Helper T cells are important because they signal the B cells to make antigens, and activate the cytotoxic T cells.

84) What planet in our solar system is most like Earth?

   A) Jupiter
   B) Venus
   C) Neptune
   D) Mars
   E) Saturn

The correct answer is D:) Mars.

85) Who has expressed origin of cell as "Omnis Cellula-e-Cellula"?

   A) Aristotle
   B) Schleiden
   C) Schwann
   D) Virchow
   E) Clapton

The correct answer is D:) Virchow.

86) Endoplasmic reticulum was discovered by

   A) Porter
   B) De Vries
   C) Sutton
   D) Watson
   E) Louis

The correct answer is A:) Porter.

87) Golgi bodies are maximum in

   A) Root cap
   B) Root tip
   C) Calyptrogen
   D) Cutin
   E) None of the above

The correct answer is C:) Calyptrogen.

88) Cytochromes contain

   A) Magnesium
   B) Manganese
   C) Copper
   D) Cobalt
   E) Iron

The correct answer is E:) Iron.

89) Meiosis is significant because

   A) There is doubling of DNA content
   B) It restores original number of chromosomes
   C) It produces identical cells
   D) It produces RBC
   E) None of the above

The correct answer is B:) It restores original number of chromosomes.

90) What is the specific name for large, open grasslands in southern Africa?

   A) Steppe
   B) Taiga
   C) Plain
   D) Veldt
   E) Plateau

The correct answer is D:) Veldt. Veldts are very similar to steppes, but the term is specific to the grasslands in southern Africa.

91) The pyrenoids are made up of

   A) Core of nucleic acid surrounded by protein sheath
   B) Core of protein surrounded by fatty sheath
   C) Proteinaceous center and starchy sheath
   D) Core of starch surrounded by sheath of protein
   E) None of the above

The correct answer is C:) Proteinaceous center and starchy sheath.

92) For the first time, the bacteria were observed by

   A) Robert Koch
   B) W.H. Stanley
   C) Louis Pasteur
   D) A.V. Leeuwenhoek
   E) Aristotle

The correct answer is D:) A.V. Leeuwenhoek.

93) Which one of the following is a sex-linked inheritance?

   A) Anemia
   B) Night blindness
   C) Colorblindness
   D) Meningitis
   E) None of the above

The correct answer is C:) Colorblindness.

94) The function of contractile vacuole in protozoa is

   A) Reproduction
   B) Locomotion
   C) Osmoregulation
   D) Digestion of food
   E) Sperm production

The correct answer is C:) Osmoregulation.

95) Which planet in our solar system has the most mass?

   A) Jupiter
   B) Saturn
   C) Earth
   D) Venus
   E) Neptune

The correct answer is A:) Jupiter.

96) The desmosomes are concerned with

   A) Cell division
   B) Cytolysis
   C) Cellular excretion
   D) Cellulose excretion
   E) Cell adherence

The correct answer is E:) Cell adherence.

97) Size of the cell is governed by

   A) Cell volume and cell surface area ratio
   B) Nucleus and cytoplasm ratio
   C) Rate of cellular metabolism
   D) All the above
   E) None of the above

The correct answer is A:) Cell volume and cell surface area ratio.

98) A polysaccharide which is synthesized and stored in liver cells is

   A) Arabinose
   B) Lactose
   C) Galactose
   D) Glycogen
   E) Cellulose

The correct answer is D:) Glycogen.

99) Each chromosome at the anaphase stage of a bone marrow cell in our body has

    A) Several chromatids
    B) No chromatids
    C) Two chromatids
    D) Only one chromatid
    E) Only one chromatid

The correct answer is C:) Two chromatids.

100) The polytene chromosomes were discovered for the first time in

    A) Chironomus
    B) Musca domestica
    C) Musca nebulo
    D) Drosophila
    E) None of the above

The correct answer is A:) Chironomus.

101) Bacterial pathogens can be controlled through:

    A) Allosteric modulation
    B) Feedback control
    C) Competitive inhibition
    D) Non-competitive inhibition
    E) None of these

The correct answer is C:) Competitive inhibition.

102) The rate at which the individuals move out of the population is called

    A) Natality
    B) Mortality
    C) Emigration
    D) Immigration
    E) None of these

The correct answer is C:) Emigration.

103) The statistical study of birth rate, mortality, migration, family size, marriage problems, ethnic groups, survival time, etc., in human beings is known as

A) Genetic counseling
B) Marriage counseling
C) Demography
D) Population graph
E) Life expectancy

The correct answer is C:) Demography.

104) In case of Reindeer moss, the growth curve is generally

A) J-shaped
B) S-shaped
C) R-shaped
D) Indefinite shape
E) D-shaped

The correct answer is A:) J-shaped.

105) The condition where the 'in vitro' fertilized ovum is brought to maturity applied by a surrogate mother is known as

A) Vitro-implantation
B) Vitro-fertilization
C) Test tube fertilization
D) Abnormal conception
E) None of these

The correct answer is B:) Vitro-fertilization.

106) The technique (prenatal diagnostic) in which a small sample of amniotic fluid is taken out from the uterus of mother to know the sex of the unborn child and also any genetic disorder is known as

   A) Chromosomal-aberration
   B) Nuclear-graphy
   C) Amniocentesis
   D) Amnio-potentiality
   E) Biotechnology

The correct answer is C:) Amniocentesis.

107) The surgical operation of vas deferens in human males to avoid flow of sperm with the semen is known as

   A) Tubectomy
   B) Vasectomy
   C) Castration
   D) Ovariectomy
   E) None of these

The correct answer is B:) Vasectomy.

108) The maximum number of individuals which the environment can support is known as

   A) Biotic potential
   B) Carrying capacity
   C) Feeding capacity
   D) Growth potential
   E) Augmentation

The correct answer is B:) Carrying capacity.

109) IUCD means

   A) Intra Urine Culture Data
   B) Inner Uterine Cellular Dose
   C) Intra Uterine Contraceptive Device
   D) Inner Urate Crystal Donor
   E) None of the above

The correct answer is C:) Intra Uterine Contraceptive Device.

110) Castration really means

   A) Removal of Prostate Gland
   B) Removal of Vas deferens
   C) Removal of Vasa efferentia
   D) Removal of Testes
   E) None of these

The correct answer is D:) Removal of Testes.

111) Which planet in our solar system is fourth from the sun?

   A) Neptune
   B) Mars
   C) Jupiter
   D) Saturn
   E) Venus

The correct answer is B:) Mars.

112) Which of the following are most convincing reasons for increasing population growth in a country?

   A) Low population of old people
   B) High birth rate
   C) Low mortality rate
   D) High population of young children
   E) Illiteracy

The correct answer is D:) High population of young children.

113) During which of the following stages does the spindle form?

   A) Anaphase
   B) Prophase
   C) Metaphase
   D) Telophase
   E) None of the above

The correct answer is B:) Prophase.

114) Which of the following is an arachnid?

   A) Butterflies
   B) Millipedes
   C) Spiders
   D) Sea urchins
   E) Clams

The correct answer is C:) Spiders.

115) The oldest fossils found on Earth are

   A) 10 million years old
   B) 100 million years old
   C) 500 million years old
   D) 1 billion years old
   E) 3 billion years old

The correct answer is E:) 3 billion years old.

116) How much of a 1600 gram sample of 68 32 Ge, whose half-life is about nine months, will remain after 4.5 years?

   A) 4 ½ grams
   B) 25 grams
   C) 50 grams
   D) 30 grams
   E) None of the above

The correct answer is B:) 25 grams. Four and a half years times twelve months is fifty-four months. 54 months divided by 9 months is 6 half-lives. Therefore, at the end of the first half-life (9 months), there is 800 grams. After the second (18 months), 400 grams. After the third (27 months), 200 grams. After the fourth (36 months), 100 grams, and after the fifth (45 months) 50 grams. And after the sixth half-life (54 months) there is 25 grams left.

117) Which of the following is an insect?

   A) Butterflies
   B) Millipedes
   C) Spiders
   D) Sea urchins
   E) Clams

The correct answer is A:) Butterflies.

118) Nuclear particles are made up from

   A) Leptons
   B) Quarks
   C) Bosons
   D) All of the above
   E) None of the above

The correct answer is B:) Quarks.

119) The prehistoric land mass that included all continents was called

   A) Foundland
   B) Pangea
   C) Gaia
   D) Iceland
   E) None of the above

The correct answer is B:) Pangea.

120) Which of the following plants are NOT representative of an arctic tundra?

   A) Lichens
   B) Mosses
   C) Sedges
   D) Dwarf shrubs
   E) All of the above are representative of an arctic tundra

The correct answer is E:) All of the above are representative of an arctic tundra. Lichens, mosses, sedges and dwarf shrubs are representative plants of an arctic tundra.

121) The gradual increase of the Earth's temperature is due to?

   A) Green Revolution
   B) Greenhouse effect
   C) Acid rain
   D) Overpopulation
   E) None of the above

The correct answer is B:) Greenhouse effect. The greenhouse effect, also known as global warming, relates to the gradual warming of the Earth's temperature.

122) Chordata refers to

   A) Exoskeleton
   B) Spinal column
   C) No bones
   D) Shellfish
   E) None of the above

The correct answer is B:) Spinal column.

123) Which of the following shows the levels of classification in order?

   A) Species, genus, family, order, class, phylum, kingdom
   B) Species, family, genus, class, order, phylum, kingdom
   C) Species, genus, class, family, order, phylum, kingdom
   D) Species, family, genus, order, class, phylum, kingdom
   E) Species, genus, family, order, phylum, class, kingdom

The correct answer is A:) Species, genus, family, order, class, phylum, kingdom.

124) The DNA molecule is shaped like

   A) Tinker toys
   B) Twisted ladder
   C) Tall h
   D) Spiral
   E) Circular

The correct answer is B:) Twisted ladder.

125) Which of the following letters is NOT used in DNA?

   A) G
   B) T
   C) D
   D) A
   E) C

The correct answer is C:) D.

126) With DNA, certain letters are always paired together. Which of the following is correct?

   A) A & C
   B) A & T
   C) A & G
   D) T & G
   E) T & C

The correct answer is B:) A & T.

127) Which of the following is NOT a part of DNA?

   A) Guanine
   B) Adenine
   C) Thymine
   D) Theramine
   E) Cytosine

The correct answer is D:) Theramine.

128) In DNA, where are proteins synthesized?

   A) Nucleus
   B) Cytoplasm
   C) RNA
   D) Mitochondria
   E) None of the above

The correct answer is B:) Cytoplasm.

129) In DNA, where does translation take place?

   A) Nucleus
   B) Cytoplasm
   C) Ribosome
   D) Mitochondria
   E) None of the above

The correct answer is C:) Ribosome.

130) There are _____ known amino acids.

   A) 4
   B) 16
   C) 20
   D) 24
   E) 30

The correct answer is C:) 20.

131) In which biome are evergreen conifers the most prominent plant?

   A) Taiga
   B) Temperate Deciduous Forest
   C) Rainforest
   D) Arctic Tundra
   E) Grassland

The correct answer is A:) Taiga. Taiga is the Russian word for forest. A taiga is frozen at least six months out of the year. Summers are very short, with only 50 to 100 days without frost.

132) Which of the following is the first phase of mitosis?

   A) Anaphase
   B) Prophase
   C) Metaphase
   D) Telophase
   E) None of the above

The correct answer is B:) Prophase.

133) Which of the following is an echinoderm?

   A) Butterflies
   B) Millipedes
   C) Spiders
   D) Sea urchins
   E) Clams

The correct answer is D:) Sea urchins.

134) During which phase does the nuclear envelope form around the two groups of daughter chromosomes?

   A) Anaphase
   B) Prophase
   C) Metaphase
   D) Telophase
   E) None of the above

The correct answer is D:) Telophase.

135) Chloroplasts are most commonly found in

   A) Roots
   B) Stems
   C) Leaves
   D) Buds
   E) Seeds

The correct answer is C:) Leaves.

136) Mitosis is when a cell is copied and its chromosome information is transferred to _____ copies of nuclei.

   A) 1
   B) 2
   C) 3
   D) 4
   E) 6

The correct answer is B:) 2.

137) Which of the following is the second phase of mitosis?

   A) Anaphase
   B) Prophase
   C) Metaphase
   D) Telophase
   E) None of the above

The correct answer is C:) Metaphase.

138) Karl von Frisch studied the communication between bees, also known as

   A) Queen bee
   B) Dance of the bees
   C) Boney hierarchy
   D) Bee agenda
   E) None of the above

The correct answer is B:) Dance of the bees.

139) Which of the following is the third phase of mitosis?

   A) Anaphase
   B) Prophase
   C) Metaphase
   D) Telophase
   E) None of the above

The correct answer is A:) Anaphase.

140) Which of the following is the fourth phase of mitosis?

   A) Anaphase
   B) Prophase
   C) Metaphase
   D) Telophase
   E) None of the above

The correct answer is D:) Telophase.

141) Which of the following means "without oxygen"?

   A) Anaerobic
   B) Aerobic
   C) Anaphase
   D) Meiosis
   E) None of the above

The correct answer is A:) Anaerobic.

142) The Miller-Urey experiment was about

   A) Simulated lighting and earth origins
   B) DNA replication
   C) Primordial soup
   D) Cell reproduction
   E) None of the above

The correct answer is A:) Simulated lighting and earth origins.

143) The largest reservoir of carbon in the world is

   A) In the mountains
   B) In the ocean
   C) In the South Pacific
   D) In North America
   E) In the atmosphere

The correct answer is B:) In the ocean.

144) What force holds your computer on your desk?

   A) Friction
   B) Relativity
   C) Strong nuclear force
   D) Electromagnetic
   E) Gravity

The correct answer is E:) Gravity.

145) In which ecosystem would a great diversity of evergreen broadleaved trees, vines, and epiphytes be expected?

   A) Prairie
   B) North American grassland
   C) Tropical rain forest
   D) Desert
   E) Temperate coniferous forest

The correct answer is C:) Tropical rain forest. An average tropical rain forest receives 50 to 260 inches of rain annually and the temperatures range from 68 to 90 degrees Fahrenheit.

146) In Pasteur's famous experiment, he discovered what?

   A) Air cannot initiate growth of microorganism
   B) Penicillin
   C) Natural selection
   D) Origin of life
   E) None of the above

The correct answer is A:) Air cannot initiate growth of microorganism.

147) What is the function of organelles?

   A) To produce hair and fingernails and support tendons.
   B) To speed up specific chemical reactions within cells.
   C) To create white blood cells which fight disease.
   D) To carry out specific cell processes.
   E) All of the above

The correct answer is D:) To carry out specific cell processes. The reason cells can be efficient is because they make use of different organelles to perform different processes. Each different organelle is responsible for a different task.

148) Charles Darwin proposed what theory?

   A) Natural selection
   B) Genetics
   C) Cloning
   D) Primordial soup
   E) None of the above

The correct answer is A:) Natural selection.

149) Charles Darwin used what animal to prove this theory?

   A) Parrot
   B) Finch
   C) Rabbit
   D) Dinosaur
   E) Dolphin

The correct answer is B:) Finch.

150) What holds everything inside the cell?

   A) Cell membrane
   B) Cytoplasm
   C) Ribosome
   D) Mitochondrion
   E) Nucleus

The correct answer is A:) Cell membrane.

151) Their function is to produce protein

   A) Cell membrane
   B) Cytoplasm
   C) Ribosome
   D) Mitochondrion
   E) Nucleus

The correct answer is C:) Ribosome.

152) Holds everything in the cell membrane

   A) Cell membrane
   B) Cytoplasm
   C) Ribosome
   D) Mitochondrion
   E) Nucleus

The correct answer is B:) Cytoplasm.

153) Responsible for breaking down sugars in the cell

   A) Cell membrane
   B) Cytoplasm
   C) Ribosome
   D) Mitochondrion
   E) Nucleus

The correct answer is D:) Mitochondrion.

154) A small network of tubes or membranes used to transfer materials throughout the cell

   A) Cell membrane
   B) Cytoplasm
   C) Ribosome
   D) Mitochondrion
   E) Nucleus

The correct answer is C:) Ribosome.

155) Which of the following is the phase that happens before mitosis begins?

   A) Interphase
   B) Prophase
   C) Metaphase
   D) Anaphase
   E) Telophase

The correct answer is A:) Interphase.

156) He is known as the Father of Genetics

   A) Thomas Malthus
   B) Gregor Mendel
   C) Harry Smith
   D) Charles Lyell
   E) Fred Hoyle

The correct answer is B:) Gregor Mendel.

157) _____ is always representative of the number of protons contained in the nucleus of an atom.

    A) Atomic number
    B) Periodic table
    C) Mass number
    D) Element
    E) Isotope

The correct answer is A:) Atomic number.

158) Which of the following is NOT true of sickle cells disease?

    A) The irregular shape in the blood cells causes the blood to flow smoother.
    B) Sickle cell disease can also be called sickle cell anemia.
    C) Sickle Hemoglobin is the name for the irregular hemoglobin of sickle cell disease.
    D) People with sickle cell disease have twisted and rigid blood cells.
    E) None of the above

The correct answer is A:) The irregular shape in the blood cells causes the blood to flow smoother. The irregular shape causes problems with blood flow, which can result in organ damage.

159) _____ an atom with the same atomic number as an element, but a different mass number.

    A) Atomic number
    B) Periodic table
    C) Mass number
    D) Element
    E) Isotope

The correct answer is E:) Isotope.

160) _____ is a classification system developed by Mendeleev.

    A) Atomic number
    B) Periodic table
    C) Mass number
    D) Element
    E) Isotope

The correct answer is B:) Periodic table.

161) _____ are atoms that all have the same atomic number.

   A) Atomic number
   B) Periodic table
   C) Mass number
   D) Element
   E) Isotope

The correct answer is E:) Isotope.

162) _____ of any atom is the number of protons plus the number of neutrons present in the nucleus of an atom.

   A) Atomic number
   B) Periodic table
   C) Mass number
   D) Element
   E) Isotope

The correct answer is C:) Mass number.

163) The transfer of energy from a body of higher temperatures to a body of lower temperature is called

   A) Work
   B) Heat
   C) 1st law of thermodynamics
   D) 2nd law of thermodynamics
   E) None of the above

The correct answer is B:) Heat.

164) Equal to force times distance is called

   A) Work
   B) Heat
   C) 1st law of thermodynamics
   D) 2nd law of thermodynamics
   E) None of the above

The correct answer is A:) Work.

165) The magnet was discovered by

   A) Thomas Malthus
   B) Gregor Mendel
   C) Harry Smith
   D) Charles Lyell
   E) Hans Christian Oersted

The correct answer is E:) Hans Christian Oersted.

166) _____ allow for the interaction of particles with one another in an electro-magnetic field.

   A) Isotope
   B) Element
   C) Photon
   D) Light
   E) None of the above

The correct answer is C:) Photon.

167) What is the layer of the atmosphere which is closest to the earth?

   A) Stratosphere
   B) Troposphere
   C) Mesosphere
   D) Ionosphere
   E) Ozone layer

The correct answer is B:) Troposphere.

168) In this part of the atmosphere, wind blows horizontally.

   A) Stratosphere
   B) Troposphere
   C) Mesosphere
   D) Ionosphere
   E) None of the above

The correct answer is A:) Stratosphere.

169) This is the part of the atmosphere where the aurora borealis occur.

   A) Stratosphere
   B) Troposphere
   C) Mesosphere
   D) Ionosphere
   E) Ozone layer

The correct answer is D:) Ionosphere.

170) To explain fine structure of the spectrum of the hydrogen atom we must consider

   A) Finite size of the nucleus
   B) The presence of neutrons in the nucleus
   C) Spin angular momentum
   D) Orbital angular momentum
   E) Nucleus size

The correct answer is C:) Spin angular momentum.

171) According to the Bohr model of the hydrogen atom, radiation is emitted when the electron

   A) Revolves in an orbit
   B) Jumps from an orbit to the nucleus
   C) Jumps from a larger orbit to a smaller orbit
   D) Jumps from a smaller orbit to a larger orbit
   E) When it is charged

The correct answer is C:) Jumps from a larger orbit to a smaller orbit.

172) For given value of n, the maximum number of electrons in an orbit can be

   A) n2
   B) 2 n2
   C) n
   D) 24
   E) 12

The correct answer is B:) 2 n2.

173) The speed of an electron in the orbit of a hydrogen atom in the ground state is

   A) c/10
   B) c/2
   C) c/137
   D) c/27
   E) None of these

The correct answer is C:) c/137.

174) The best laboratory approximation to an ideal black body is

   A) A lump of charcoal heated to a high temperature
   B) A glass surface coated with coal tar
   C) A metallic piece coated with a black dye
   D) A hollow enclosure blackened inside with soot and having a small hole
   E) Both B and C

The correct answer is D:) A hollow enclosure blackened inside with soot and having a small hole.

175) Light from a distant star is examined with a spectroscope. The spectrum shows

   A) Chemical composition of star
   B) Temperature of star
   C) Distance of star from earth
   D) Both A and B
   E) None of the above

The correct answer is B:) Temperature of star.

Test-Taking Strategies

Here are some test-taking strategies that are specific to this test and to other CLEP tests in general:

- Keep your eyes on the time. Pay attention to how much time you have left.
- Read the entire question and read all the answers. Many questions are not as hard to answer as they may seem. Sometimes, a difficult sounding question really only is asking you how to read an accompanying chart. Chart and graph questions are on most CLEP tests and should be an easy free point.
- If you don't know the answer immediately, the new computer-based testing lets you mark questions and come back to them later if you have time.
- Read the wording carefully. Some words can give you hints to the right answer. There are no exceptions to an answer when there are words in the question such as "always" "all" or "none." If one of the answer choices includes most or some of the right answers, but not all, then that is not the answer. Here is an example:

    The primary colors include all of the following:
    A) Red, Yellow, Blue, Green
    B) Red, Green, Yellow
    C) Red, Orange, Yellow
    D) Red, Yellow, Blue
    E) None of the above

    Although item A includes all the right answers, it also includes an incorrect answer, making it incorrect. If you didn't read it carefully, was in a hurry, or didn't know the material well, you might fall for this.
- Make a guess on a question that you do not know the answer to. There is no penalty for an incorrect answer. Eliminate the answer choices that you know are incorrect. For example, this will let your guess be a 1 in 3 chance instead.

What Your Score Means

Based on your score, you may, or may not, qualify for credit at your specific institution. At University of Phoenix, a score of 50 is passing for full credit. At Utah Valley University, the score is unpublished, the school will accept credit on a case-by-case basis. Another school, Brigham Young University (BYU) does not accept CLEP credit.

To find out what score you need for credit, you need to get that information from your school's website or academic advisor.

You can score between 20 and 80 on any CLEP test. Some exams include percentile ranks. Each correct answer is worth one point. You lose no points for unanswered or incorrect questions.

 Test Preparation

How much you need to study depends on your knowledge of a subject area. If you are interested in literature, took it in school, or enjoy reading then your studying and preparation for the literature or humanities test will not need to be as intensive as for someone who is new to literature.

This book is much different than the regular CLEP study guides. This book actually teaches you the information that you need to know to pass the test. If you are particularly interested in an area, or feel like you want more information, do a quick search online. There is a lot you'll need to memorize. Almost everything in this book will be on the test. It is important to understand all major theories and concepts listed in the table of contents. It is also very important to know any bolded words.

Don't worry if you do not understand or know a lot about the area. If you study hard, you can complete and pass the test.

To prepare for the test, make a series of goals. Set aside a certain amount of time to review the information you have already studied and to learn additional material. Take notes as you study-it will help you learn the material.

 Legal Note

All rights reserved. This Study Guide, Book and Flashcards are protected under US Copyright Law. No part of this book or study guide or flashcards may be reproduced, distributed or stored in a retrieval system, or transmitted in any form or by any means, electronic, mechanical, photocopying, recording, or otherwise, without the prior written permission of the publisher Breely Crush Publishing, LLC. This manual is not supported by or affiliated with the College Board, creators of the CLEP test. CLEP is a registered trademark of the College Entrance Examination Board, which does not endorse this book.

References

Reprinted with Permission.
[1]http://www.albinism.org/publications/what_is_albinism.html

FLASHCARDS

This section contains flashcards for you to use to further your understanding of the material and test yourself on important concepts, names or dates. Read the term or question then flip the page over to check the answer on the back. Keep in mind that this information may not be covered in the text of the study guide. Take your time to study the flashcards, you will need to know and understand these concepts to pass the test.

| Louis Pasteur | Primordial Soup Theory |

| John Haldane | Alexander Oparin |

| Fred Hoyle | Creationism |

| Evolution | Karl von Linné |

Molecules interacting at random to create compounds that would result in life	Biologist
Primoridial Soup Theory	Primoridial Soup Theory
Theory that the world was created by God	Interstellar Theory: life was developed in interstellar clouds
Botanist - pea plan hybrids	Theory that humans evolved from other organisms on earth

George Louis Leclerc

Comte de Buffon

Erasmus Darwin

Charles Lamarck

George Cuvier

Charles Lyel

Darwin's famous experiment included

Cell Membrane

Thought that the world was older than 6000 years	Believed in evolution
First scientist to publicly declare evolution	Grandfather of Charles Darwin
Proved that forces changing the shape of the earth's surface must have been operating in the past much the same way as they are now idea referred to as uniformitarianism	First scientist to document extinct species
Holds all the stuff that is supposed to be in the cell inside the cell	Finches from the Galápagos Islands

Cytoplasm	Ribosomes
Mitochondrion	Eukaryotes
Prokaryotes	5 Stages of Mitosis
Interphase	Prophase

Produce protein	Holds the nucleus in eukaryotes, plus all other cellular components with the cell membrane
Cells in animals and humans	Components responsible for breaking down sugars entering the cell into energy
Interphase, Prophase, Metaphase, Anaphase, Telephase	Cells in bacteria and cyanophytes
During phase one, the DNA and proteins in the cell begin to condense, the microtubules are assembled and move to opposite ends of the nucleus, and the nuclear envelope begins to break up.	This phase actually occurs prior to phase one of mitosis. During interphase, the cell grows larger.

Metaphase	Anaphase
Meiosis	DNA is made up of what four bases?
Humans have how many chromosomes?	Transcription
Translation	Name Charles Darwin's Ship

During this phase, the attachment between the two chromatids of each chromosome break off and become separate chromosomes, which move to opposite poles of the spindle

During metaphase, the microtubules break through the nucleus and create a spindle apparatus, attaching to sister chromatids of each chromosome. All the chromosomes line up at the equator of the spindle, condensing as much as possible.

adenine (A), thymine (T), guanine (G), and cytosine (C)

Meiosis is the type of the cell division that results in "germ cells," or eggs and sperm

First step interpreting information stored in genes. Copies of the info in DNA made. The copy of the DNA is called "messenger RNA" or "mRNA." RNA is similar to DNA in that it is also an information coding molecule

22

HMS Beagle

To make proteins in the cell, the mRNA attaches itself to the cell's ribosomes, which are capable of reading genetic information, and in turn create proteins, a process known as translation.

What bird helped Darwin realize natural selection?	Natural Selection
Gregor Mendel	In genetics, Upper case letters mean what? (ex. PP)
Chromosomes come in what?	Chromosomes carry what?
Somatic Cell	How many chromosomes to a set?

When nature determines what will evolve and what will not survive	Finch
Upper case mean dominant, lower case means recessive	Father of Genetics
Genes	Pairs
46	Full set of chromosomes

Cloning	Gametes
How many gametes do you need for reproduction?	Zygote
Hemophilia	Disorders that can be passed on
Polygenetic	Rh Factor

Reproductive cells	Reproducing using just the somatic cell
Two fused gametes, the first part of a human	2
Colorblindness, Hemophilia, Muscular Dystrophy	Blood clotting disorder
Presence or absence of protein	Genes that determine what is passed on

Cells reproduce what?	Chromosomes act as a template in what?
DNA stands for what?	DNA molecules consist of how many chains?
How many pairs of chromosomes determine sex?	How many pairs are there in a chromosome?
How many total chromosomes is there in a nucleus?	Ribosome

Cell reproduction	Themselves
Two chains	Deoxyribonucleic Acid
23	One, X & Y
Organelle	46

What percentage of the body is water?	Carbohydrates are
Proteins are	Fats
Scurvy	Yeast is what?
Louis Pasteur	Malaria

Sugar and starches	0.9
Storage area for food	Sources of essential amino acids
Alive and an animal	Lack of vitamin C
Disease spread mostly by mosquitoes	Father of Microbiology

DDT	**Virus**
Virus Examples	**Trichinosis**
Cancer	**Benign Tumor**
Malignant Tumor	**Hypertension**

Protein that mimics RNA and DNA	Chemical used to kill mosquitoes, harmful to humans
Parasite eggs in the muscles of animals	Colds, AIDS, Herpes, Flu, Measles
Cancer restricted to an area	Genetic material that is damaged and causes sporadic cell growth
High Blood Pressure	Unrestricted Cancer cell growth

Atherosclerosis	**Plaque**
Leukemia	**Exhale**
Thyroid regulates what?	**What glands give the "Fight or Flight" response?**
Leukocytes	**Erythrocytes**

Built up substances in the arteries	Hardened arteries
Breathing out carbon dioxide	Form of cancer where you have too many white blood cells
Adrenal glands	Metabolism
Red blood cells	White blood cells that fight infection

Four Major Muscle Tissue Types	**Three Types of Muscle Tissue**
Smooth Muscle Examples	**Skeletal Muscle Examples**
Cardiac	**Hepatic Portal Circulation**
Urea	**Uric Acid**

Smooth, Skeletal, Cardiac	Epithelial, Connectiver, Nervous, Muscle
Striated, around skeleton	Veins and arteries
Regulates sugar level	Heart muscle
Paste like feces of birds and reptiles	Nitrogenous waste of humans

Ecotherms

Endotherm

Warm Blooded

Cold Blooded

Endocrine System

Cornea

Echolocation

Pheromones

Warm blooded animals	Cold blooded animals
Animals who need warm climate because they do not regulate their body temperature	Animals who regulate their own body temperature
Protective covering of the eye	Glands that produce hormones for major glands
Scents that insects use to communicate with each other	Ultrasound that animals (bats) use to navigate

Social Insect Example	Which cell (animal or
Molecules are the building blocks of what?	Atomic Number
Periodic Table of Elements	Mass Number
Element	Isotope

Plants	Bees, Ants
In the periodic table of elements, the atomic number is always representative of the number of protons contained in the nucleus of an atom	Any living cell
The mass number of any atom is the number of protons plus the number of neutrons present int he nucleus of an atom. In other words, mass number equals the total number of particles present in the nucleus.	The periodic table of elements is a classification system developed by a man named Mendeleev based upon the chemical properties of elements
An isotope is an atom with the same atomic number as an element, but a different mass number	Elements are atoms that all have the same atomic number

Fusion	**Fission**
Scientific Method – 4 Steps	**Covalent Bond**
Combination or Synthesis Reaction	**Decomposition**
Single Replacement	**Double Replacement**

A nuclear reaction that results in the splitting of a heavier nucleus into two lighter nuclei first atomic bomb	Two light nuclei (with a relatively small atomic mass) combine to form a single, heavier nucleus - example - nuclear plants
Chemical bond in which electrons are shared between atoms	1. Gather information, 2. Generate Hypothesis, 3. Test Hypothesis, 4. Revise
Decomposition is a chemical reaction where a compound breaks down into two or more simpler substances	This reaction is the result of two or more substances uniting to create a compound
A double replacement reaction is a reaction between two compounds in which elements or ions replace one another	This type of reaction results when one element replaces another in a compound

Work	Thermodynamics Law #1
Thermodynamics Law #2	Four States of Matter
Einstein's Law of Special Relativity	William Watson
Thomas Young	Photon

Energy can be neither created nor destroyed. It can be converted, but you cannot increase the amount of energy in the universe or decrease it. The second part of the first law is that the change in internal energy of any system is equal to heat plus work.	Work is equal to force times distance
Solids, liquids, gases, and plasmas	There is a finite amount of energy in the universe, its quality is degraded irreversibly. Every time a chemical reaction takes place, part of the energy required to do the work is transformed into some other form than that which helped perform the work.
Experimented with electricity	Neither distance nor time are absolute
Particles communicating forces between charged particles. They are what allow for one another in an electomagnetic field	Studied light in 1803 and determined that light was a wave of motion

Speed of Light	Electromagnetic Radiation
High Frequency Sound	Age of the universe?
Spiral Galaxies	Elliptical Galaxies
Irregular Galaxies	Nebular Hypothesis

This radiation is a combination of oscillating electric magnetic fields. They are normally perpendicular to each other through space and carry energy from one place to another. Light is one form of electromagnetic radiation.	The speed of light is the speed with which one photon travels through time and space. In a vacuum, a photon will travel 3x108 m/s-1.
12 billion years	"high pitched"
Elliptical galaxies are much more common than spiral galaxies, and usually do not have a disk in the center. That means that no new stars are forming.	Spiral galaxies are similar to the Milky Way where our earth resides. They have a bulge and a disk where stars form, and two or more arms winding out from the central disk.
A large cloud of dust in our galaxy called a nebula began to collapse from the pressure of the gravitational forces exerted upon it, resulting in the creation of our solar system	They are basically any galaxies that are not either spiral or elliptical

www.ingramcontent.com/pod-product-compliance
Lightning Source LLC
Chambersburg PA
CBHW081825300426
44116CB00014B/2491